Self-Publishing Lesbian Fiction

ELIZABETH ANDRE

Self-Publishing Lesbian Fiction

Elizabeth Andre

For inquiries about self-publishing consulting, workshops, or other questions, contact tulabellaruby@gmail.com

ISBN: 9798868943010

tulabellarubypress

Disclaimer: Mentioning a person or company does not mean they endorse me or I endorse them, although I've tried to avoid mentioning anyone horrible. It also says nothing about their sexuality or how they identify. They may be LGBTQ+. They may not be.

Conflict of interest statement: No one has paid me to be mentioned in my book. I've only named people and organizations that I've either had direct experience with or those I've heard very good things about from people and organizations I trust.

Editor: Cassandra Pierce

Note: Self-publishing changes all the time. To keep on top of things, scan this QR code to subscribe to my Substack, The Lesfic Self-Publisher.

DEDICATION

Dedicated to everyone who knows they have a story within them and is willing to share that story with the world

SELF-PUBLISHING LESBIAN FICTION

ELIZABETH ANDRE

A step-by-step guide for successfully writing and self-publishing lesbian, Sapphic, WLW, queer, and other fun fiction!

Write and self-publish your novel in e-book, print, and audiobook formats. I can show you how.

I'm an award-winning bestselling lesbian fiction author, and I've been writing and self-publishing fiction since 2014. I've learned a lot on this journey, and I've put it all in this book including:

- Publishing your book for little or no money
- How to make money from your novel
- Why self-publishing is a great option for those who write lesbian, Sapphic, WLW, or queer fiction
- Tips for completing your novel and becoming a better writer
- How to work with editors and cover designers
- Formatting your book and getting it ready to publish
- Mastering marketing even if you hate it
- Navigating the growing list of publishing platforms available for self-published authors
- How to get your book into bookstores

I have been self-publishing lesbian fiction since 2014. I write cozy paranormal mystery, lesbian romance, science fiction, and young adult stories. Before turning my hand to fiction, I was a newspaper reporter for many years, and I have the paper cuts to prove it. I have won many writing awards including a Goldie from the Golden Crown Literary Society for fiction and a Peter Lisagor Award from the Chicago Headline Club for journalism. I am a lesbian in an interracial same-sex marriage living in the Midwest.

SELF-PUBLISHING LESBIAN FICTION

Part I: Adventures in writing and self-publishing lesbian fiction

Part II: The nuts and bolts of self-publishing lesbian fiction

Part III: The adventure continues

ACKNOWLEDGMENTS

Thank you to our beta readers Jennifer, Marc, Liz, Julie, Jennifer, Lana, and Kamala for making this book so much better.

A note about lesbian fiction and what it includes

Over the years, various controversies have erupted over what should be included under the lesbian fiction umbrella. Ask ChatGPT to define the word lesbian, and it will write, "lesbian is a term used to describe a woman who is emotionally, romantically, or sexually attracted to other women. It is a sexual orientation and refers to a woman's identity and experiences in relation to same-sex attraction." Does the lesbian fiction umbrella include trans women? Of course. Does it include people who are non-binary? Sure. What about bisexuals and pansexuals and asexuals? Sure.

This book is not a dictionary or a position paper. If you include yourself under the lesbian umbrella, come on in. If you write fiction that you believe belongs under the lesbian fiction umbrella, come on in. If you would prefer to use the term "women loving women," cool. If you prefer the term "Sapphic," go for it. "Queer" is a word a lot of people like. I hope you get something out of this book that moves you closer to your dreams.

PART I: ADVENTURES IN WRITING AND SELF-PUBLISHING LESBIAN FICTION

CHAPTER ONE

Why self-publish lesbian fiction?

I know you.

You like to read. You like to tell stories. You have a dream of holding a book in your hands with your name (or your favorite pen name) on the cover. You dream of someday seeing someone on the bus or maybe at an airport, and they're reading your book. Maybe you want to see your book on the shelf at your local bookstore with a tag that says, "local author." Or maybe you want a book to give to your mom, something with your name on it, and she'll tell you how proud of you she is.

Whatever your dream, it involves a story that you must tell and a book that you must send out into the world. I know what scares you. What if everyone hates it? Worse yet, what if no one reads it?

What if someone laughs at you?

I know you've also heard all of the conventional wisdom about book publishing. It's expensive (usually said by someone who has never written a book, let alone published one). It's hard (It can be, but it doesn't have to be). You must have an agent (not true). No one wants to publish lesbian books, and no one wants to read them.

SO WRONG

The worst writing advice I was ever given was offered up by a friend in high school who, when he learned that I wanted to write books, advised me to get myself kidnapped and write a book about the experience. He believed that book would really sell.

I did not attempt to follow that advice, but over the past decade I have written and self-published a couple dozen lesbian fiction books. I've been selling lesbian fiction in paperback, e-book, and hardcover, and I've sold a lot of books. I have fans. I have superfans. I recently met a reader in the wild who, unprompted, revealed that she had read one of my books and enjoyed it. I've just started making audiobooks and serializing my fiction on various apps. Traditional large publishing houses may not have much interest in lesbian fiction, although there are some smaller houses with strong lesbian imprints. Readers, however, are definitely interested in lesbian books. They buy them, and they read them.

Conventional wisdom has failed me regularly. Your mileage may vary.

Bottom line: never take advice from people who have not walked the walk. Do not take advice about running a marathon from someone who does not run. Do not take advice about a city you are about to visit from someone who has never been there.

Take advice about self-publishing lesbian fiction from people like me who have done it and done it a lot. I've learned so much over the past decade, and I'm putting it all in this book. Maybe you'll learn something. Maybe you'll have more fun making the same mistakes I did. In any case, I hope this book gives you what you need to achieve your goals and make your dreams come true.

I hope you write and self-publish your book. The more lesbian books there are, the more books readers will buy written by people like you and me.

Lesbian fiction is a genre that has grown tremendously in popularity in recent years and for good reason. It offers us representation. It gives us validation. In romance fiction, we are guaranteed a happy ending. In mystery fiction, we get to solve the crime. In science fiction we save whole planets. We get to be the heroes of our own stories in every genre. Online bookstores offer up hundreds of thousands of lesbian books written by thousands of authors. Brick-and-mortar bookstores have a more limited selection, but, depending on the bookstore, those lesbian fiction shelves can be bursting at the seams.

Imagine your book there.

So, why not go with a traditional publisher? Why not get an agent? Why spend time self-publishing if you just want to write?

It's a myth that if you sign with an agent or a traditional publisher, all you'll have to do is write and they will take care of the rest. With a traditional publisher, you still have to market your book. You still have to do a lot of the work that you have to do if you self-publish your baby. We all have choices about how we can spend our time. Do you want to spend your time sending your book to publishers and agents or do you want to publish and send your book out into the world?

An author recently posted on Twitter that after they had been dropped by an agent, they didn't write for three months. Don't give someone else that much power over your life and your craft. It's not worth it.

Still want the validation that you think traditional publishing will provide? An editor who tells you how great your writing is? An agent who tells you how fabulous you are?

Here's some validation. When you need it, return to this part of the book:

You are such a good writer that it's a crime not to share your story (or stories) with the world. The world

wants your story. The world needs your story, now more than ever.

Self-publishing is not a second choice or a last chance for writers rejected by the ever-shrinking traditional publishing world. It's a fabulous choice for those of us who want to take good care of our babies (our books), control our work, and take charge of our destiny. This is especially true for those of us who want to write, publish, and sell stories that traditional publishing isn't that interested in, like a love story featuring explicit sex between two 65-year-old women that addresses the very real issue of vaginal dryness (*Right Time for Love* by me). Or how about a cozy paranormal mystery featuring a Black lesbian and Jewish lesbian who don't like each other very much, then date, and end up launching and running a paranormal detective agency together (*Paranormal Grievance Committee Chronicles* by me again)?

> *"The act of self-publishing a novel is a badge*
> *of honor, evidence of remarkable discipline,*
> *and an illustration of a rarely celebrated*
> *resourcefulness."—Eddie S. Pierce Jr., owner*
> *of Rainbow Room Publishing*

Self-publishing addresses some of the biases that have plagued traditional publishing for decades. Research carried out by WordsRated, a non-commercial, international research data and analytics group, found that 67% of top-rated, self-published books are written by women, compared to just 39% of traditionally published books. With regard to lesbian books, self-published books dominate the lesbian fiction bestseller lists on Amazon. Self-publishing levels the playing field, and there is opportunity for everyone.

You, yes you, can self-publish a book without going broke or spending all of your time on it. You can publish something that you can be proud of. You can publish something that other people will want to buy and read.

Over the past decade self-publishing has become a behemoth. About a third of all e-books are self-published, according to WordsRated. Approximately $1.25 billion worth of self-published books are sold each year, and Amazon pays $520 million in royalties to self-published authors annually.

So, how much money can you make? Self-publishing is not a get rich quick scheme. You have to do some work, although most of it is pretty fun. Some self-published authors make a living. Others make six figures. A few make seven. The average self-published author makes about $1,000 a year, and those numbers are better than the average traditionally published author. According to the Alliance of Independent Authors, incomes for self-published authors have been going up over the past decade while incomes for traditionally published authors have been going down.

"Even in the worst of times, there's always someone who makes money. There's no reason that person can't be you."—my dad.

If you want to try the traditional publishing route, have a good time. Don't say you weren't warned. There may still be information in this book for you. Even if you work with a traditional publisher, you should know how publishing works, and you have to do your own marketing anyway. This book will be especially useful to you if you end up deciding traditional publishing wasn't all you expected it to be. In this book, I explore the world of self-publishing in the context of lesbian fiction in all its glory. I discuss writing, preparing the manuscript, the publishing process, marketing and promotion strategies, and best practices, all within the context of identifying and meeting your goals. I mostly focus on my own experience but include the experiences of others as appropriate. There is more than one way to do self-publishing right, and what works for me may not work for you. You have to decide what's right for you based on who you are and your goals.

Self-publishing can seem daunting at first, but it offers many advantages for writers. You have creative control. You can publish faster, and you get to keep your money. You don't have to share.

Key point: You don't have to do everything perfectly for your first book. You can learn as you go. Each book will be better written and better produced. And you don't have to do everything with your first book. You can constantly expand vendors and platforms as your book catalog grows and your skills improve.

It takes years to become an overnight sensation, and you may even become a better writer in the process. I know I did.

Whether you are a seasoned writer looking to explore self-publishing options or a beginner who is just starting out, this book is designed to provide you with the tools, knowledge, and inspiration you need to identify and achieve your goals. So, let's dive into the world of self-publishing and explore the endless possibilities that await you as a lesbian fiction writer.

Note of caution: Traditional publishing is shrinking, but hybrid publishing is growing. In traditional publishing, authors are paid a share of royalties. In hybrid publishing, authors pay to publish. They may or may not receive a share of royalties. There are some hybrid publishers who charge reasonable prices for their services. They are honest and upfront about what they do and what they can achieve. They operate in line with the criteria outlined by the Independent Book Publishers Association. There are also some hybrid publishers that are far more predatory, charging exorbitant rates for poor quality work and making promises that they cannot possibly fulfill. Always remember that self-publishing puts the writer in charge. While it is appropriate to pay for editing, proofing, cover design, and marketing services, you get to decide which ones to use and how much you will pay. There are many ways to complete parts of the process inexpensively, and remember, you can always improve a book and create a second edition with all the bells and whistles that you couldn't do with the first edition. Modern publishing with e-book and print on demand mean improvements are always possible.

Before working with any company, check them out. I recommend typing the company name into Google or some other search engine followed by the words "hate" or "scam." This will make the negative information about them pop up. Writer Beware® is a phenomenal resource run by the Science Fiction & Fantasy Writers Association. Check to see if they've written about your potential partner before signing anything.

I know I said that there are several ways to do self-publishing right. Going into debt to do so and letting someone else hurt your baby (your book), that's doing it wrong.

A note about how to use this book: Each chapter can stand alone. You can read this book from cover to cover, but feel free to dip into the chapters that are most relevant to you as needed. Chapters One through Eleven talk about writing and self-publishing in a general way and include some of my best stories about writing and self-publishing lesbian fiction. Chapters Twelve through Twenty focus on the nuts and bolts of each platform. Use those chapters as needed. Chapters Twenty-one through Twenty-four wrap everything up, and I end with the reasons why you should be proud of yourself and the terrible advice people insist on giving writers.

You should be so proud of yourself for just starting this journey. I know I'm proud of you.

CHAPTER TWO

My lesbian fiction self-publishing journey

When I started writing LGBTQ fiction in 2014, I wrote m/m romance. Why? Well, I had some experience with it. I'd written some in the 1990s. Hey, it was a living. When I decided to write fiction featuring same-sex couplings in 2014, I turned to m/m fiction because what I read online—in Facebook groups and from a grad school friend who was already writing m/m romance—it sold better than lesbian romance. Indeed, the lists of bestsellers in the LGBTQ category on Amazon reflected this sentiment. I began writing my first m/m romance, *5 Easy Chocolate Pieces*. It was published by the same small press that was publishing my friend.

I wrote more m/m romances, but in early 2015, I decided I wanted to write a lesbian romance, or f/f as I put it in an email to my old grad school friend. "I mean, like a fun romp. I wouldn't want it to be angsty or too lesbian process heavy," I wrote in that email. From that came *Love's Perfect Vintage*, the first of what would become 13 Lesbian Light Reads stories. My wife who writes with me was

12

skeptical (FYI: Elizabeth Andre is two people who write together; my wife and I). She wasn't convinced that lesbian stuff would sell. I, on the other hand, was convinced that it would sell. My reasoning was that there wasn't enough of the kind of stories I wanted to write and read: light, fun, low on the angst meter. Most importantly, it had a happy ending, something everyone deserves.

Unsurprisingly, I liked writing the lesbian stories so much better than the m/m ones, but we kept writing the m/m ones even after we started publishing our books ourselves. I think we still had stories to tell through that m/m lens. The ideas for lesfic stories came thick and fast, though. Some of them ended up as books we went on to self-publish, like the idea of a 21st century African American woman slipping into early 20th century England and how she manages to live and love there until she can figure out how to get back home (*The Time Slip Girl*). Watching the TV show *Supernatural* is where I got the idea for a series of books featuring two lesbian ghost hunters and detailing their adventures with the occult and the unknown (*Paranormal Grievance Committee Chronicles* series). One story that I still have a soft spot for is one I came up with from a writing exercise I found on another author's blog. The novella I wrote based on that idea tells the story of a juvenile delinquent a couple of centuries in the future who dreams of fighting a kaiju (*Taijiku*).

Since the team behind Elizabeth Andre is an interracial couple, it was important that the lesfic stories I wrote have, as much as possible, couples like us. Most of the books I read in childhood and as a young adult didn't have much variety when it came to protagonists. I was and am an imaginative, empathetic person, so being able to see myself in a protagonist who I had next to nothing in common with wasn't difficult. I did often wish that I didn't have to work quite so hard to find something relatable about a main character. As the saying goes, representation matters.

And 30 books later, here we are…

More than anything else, if you want to write your stories, do it. Don't pass up the opportunity to tell your stories, whether they're romance, westerns set in the far future, an archaeological dig in a sci-fi setting, a hard-boiled crime novel, or sexy, thrilling suspense. This book can help you publish those stories, if that is your dream.

CHAPTER THREE

Writing a book

The first step in preparing to self-publish a book is writing it. I recommend writing a good one and not writing your marketing plan before you've written your book. Do not build a giant following on a particular social media platform until you have something to sell them. Remember a key piece of advice from the dance world. If you want to do ballet, start by putting on your tights. If you start with the tutu, you'll never get the tights on.

Start writing your book. Apply your butt to a chair, or follow Ernest Hemingway's example and stand. Write on your phone, a laptop, paper, or your preferred medium. I have a dedicated writing spot in my home. I write there on my laptop, except when it's too cold. Then I write on my sewing table in my craft room or on a table in the living room. Sometimes I write on my phone on public transportation. Sometimes I write at the beach. I write every day, except when I don't.

Don't let the perfect get in the way of the good.

What should you write?

Let's back up for a moment. What should you write? Where do you get ideas?

I used to say that I got my ideas from Kmart, especially when they had blue light specials on them, but that retailer barely exists anymore. The truth of the matter is that ideas are like air. They are all around you, and your imagination is a muscle that needs to be strong enough to catch them. Maybe it's gotten flabby over the years? Maybe adulthood made things too serious? If you want to write a book, it's time to workout.

Remember: If you're out of running shape, you don't start by running a marathon. Try walking around the block.

"Creativity is intelligence having fun"—
Albert Einstein

To truly set your imagination free, I recommend *The Artist's Way* by Julia Cameron. I also recommend a few exercises that work for me. These can prevent your writing from getting stale, keep things fun, and keep you writing.

Exercise 1: Look up from your reading. Make up a story about something or someone you see. You don't have to write it down or tell anyone about it. Actually, I advise against telling anyone your idea initially. Let your imagination run wild, like a child who's been given a new box of crayons and a blank sheet of paper.

If it helps, buy yourself a new box of crayons and a whole ream of blank sheets of paper. You're an adult now. You can do that.

Example: I'm writing this in a conference room in a downtown Chicago high rise. It's a sunny spring day, but (and here's where the fun starts) I look out the window. A crack is slowly starting to appear down the middle of the Hancock building. The building is still standing, but no one else seems to see it. I call my wife. She works on the 77th floor of the Hancock, seemingly where the crack begins. The phone rings but then goes dead. Then the sky goes dark.

You can have that idea if you want. I'm not using it, and I have loads more.

Do the same thing the next day. Don't tell anyone your idea until you're ready. Beware of anyone who says, "that's not original," or "that's not realistic." Those are not useful comments. You should not be sharing your precious ideas with anyone who says those kinds of things. There is no such thing as an original idea, and who needs reality? We're writing fiction here, people! We're looking for suspension of disbelief. We're creating a whole new world to play in.

My father, a pulp novelist in the 1960s, always told me, "Bad writers borrow, good writers steal."

Versions of this statement have been attributed to T.S. Eliot, Pablo Picasso, and Oscar Wilde. Feel free to steal it and call it your own, just like my dad did.

Exercise 2: Do something different. This can be large or small. Size doesn't matter. Have ketchup with your fries if that's not what you usually do. Write about what it feels like to have ketchup on your fries. Maybe in order to have ketchup, you have to ask a beautiful woman to pass you the bottle. Your fingers touch for a moment. Your eyes lock. You talk about ketchup. Then you talk about tomato farmers. Everything she says is so smart that you can't leave, and you don't until the restaurant turns out the lights and kicks you out.

You can have that idea too.

Set your alarm five minutes early. Use that time to stare out the window. Take the other way home, the way that you don't usually take. Say "yes" to someone you usually say "no" to, especially if that person is yourself.

Exercise 3: Take a memory and rewrite the ending.

When I was in college, I interviewed a beauty pageant contestant for the student newspaper. She called me after the story ran and wanted to go out for coffee. Because I had a hard time believing someone so beautiful would want to hang out with me and I'm an idiot, I said, "no." I never saw her again, and I don't know where she is. Many years later, I wrote the story, *The Beauty Queen Called Twice*, which was all about us reconnecting, making out, falling in love, and living happily ever after.

You can write the story of the life you wanted to have.

Exercise 4: Take three objects, places, and/or concepts—for example, a motorcycle, a grain silo, and something talking that shouldn't talk—and write a flash fiction story (300-1,500 words) about them.

Exercise 5: Think about the book you'd like to read. Try to find it. If it doesn't exist, you're going to have to write it.

Exercise 6: Play with your ideas like a kitten plays with a ball of string. If you don't have any toys, get some. I like modeling clay and crayons. Choose a toy that calls to you, maybe even a real ball of string. Consider involving trusted friends or family at this stage but make it very clear that you are not seeking criticism. You are not creating a critique group. This is an opportunity to expand your idea. You are asking them to add to your idea. Discard nothing. Truly listen to each other. Ask for what you need. Take notes. If you do not finish the ideation session energized and ready to write, don't ever ideate with those people again.

The ideation and writing stages are great opportunities to identify who is a safe person with whom to share your ideas (they nod and cheer you on, no matter what you say) and those who are not safe (they pick apart and criticize your ideas in any way, shape, or form). You can still have the latter group in your life. There are some things you just can't share with them.

Note: "Write what you know" is terrible advice. You should write what you want to read. I was once on a panel at a convention discussing writing about love and sex. I was on the panel with my wife, and we were writing gay male fiction at the time. (I'm so glad we were able to give that up.) Other people on the panel included a lesbian who wrote heterosexual romance, an asexual woman who wrote gay male romance, and a gay man who wrote furry mysteries. Furries are individuals who are especially interested in anthropomorphic or cartoon animals. They may dress up as furry animals. I know there are controversies around appropriation and what that actually means. I address that in Chapter Five but write the story you have inside you. I know it's there.

Start writing it. Write some more.

The only way to become a writer is to write. The only way to become a better writer is to write more. You have to write badly before you write well.

A note about writing classes: There are loads of them. They are in person, online, and by mail. There are also loads of books about writing of varying quality.

The only way to become a better writer is to write more. If your chosen writing class or book means you write more, that's great. You should continue it. If your writing class is led by someone who sneers at you, makes a snide comment if you misplace a comma, or makes you feel badly about yourself or what you've written, don't ever go back. I don't care if you can't get a refund. Protect your dream at all costs.

"When you give up your dream, you die."—
Nick, the movie Flashdance

A note for people who misplace commas all the time and for whom grammar is not a strength but who want to write: Of course, you can still be a writer, but you need to develop strategies and use tools that improve your skills. Bad grammar and punctuation can take a reader out of the story. You want to avoid that at all costs. You want to keep the reader in your story as much as possible. Never forget your reader and always be nice to them. Take grammar classes, use tools such as Grammarly or ProWritingAid to improve your writing, and write in a way that is best for you. That may mean utilizing speech-to-text tools. Maybe you need a font specifically designed for those with dyslexia? Only you know the tools you need to truly write well, and I know you have it in you.

Important: You can't get to a great final draft without a bad first draft. Writing that first draft is a critical step on the journey to creating a final draft. However, never publish that first draft. Publish the final draft.

A note on the difference between style and grammar: It is very important to know the difference. There are some things in English that are just plain wrong.

Example: I were waiting for the shop to closed.

That was painful to write.

Then there are things that are incorrect because of circumstance. Circumstances include different countries, different dialects, different stylebooks, and different audiences.

Example: The adviser spoke about money, investments and goals.

That example sentence is correct if you are using an Associated Press stylebook, which is primarily used by journalists. "Adviser" is spelled with an "e," and there is no Oxford comma (the serial comma before a conjunction).

Stylebooks rule. I don't care what your third-grade teacher taught you. Choose a stylebook and stick to it. Or not. You can also choose an editor who sticks to a stylebook you like.

Another example: My favourite colour is purple.

That example sentence is correct if you are writing English in the United Kingdom and most Commonwealth countries. It is not correct in American English.

If this is too much detail for you to care about, if it scares you in any way, don't worry about it. Don't get hung up on revising or editing yet. Leave that for Chapter Five. Now is the time to just write. Let those words flow out of you. You can revise and edit later.

You can't edit a blank page.

For me to write, I need the ability to be able to write anywhere and in a crowd, which is why I love writing on my phone using Google Docs on the bus or the train, at the beach, at a health fair where I've volunteered to help out with HIV testing, wherever. I can write anywhere. That is not the way many people write. That's okay. It's the way I write.

You be you. Use the tools available. Maybe develop the tools you need. Someone else may need them too.

A comment on using generative AI tools such as ChatGPT or Bard: Controversies are raging about the various generative AI tools that have emerged. These are tools. If you need them, use them. If you enjoy them, use them. The initial outline for this book was created by ChatGPT. That seven-chapter outline was so inspiring to me that I used it to create a better 24-chapter outline and write this book. I have used ChatGPT for inspiration, brainstorming, and getting organized, much like I've also used internet searches, but I spent months writing this book.

Note: AI can stand for artificial intelligence or augmented intelligence.

Also note: Anything created by AI cannot be copyrighted and is in the public domain. This means the original seven-chapter outline for this book is not copyrighted. However, everything I've written is subject to copyright. This book is copyrighted by me.

Back to how to improve your writing….

While the best way to be a better writer is to write more, here are some tips.

1. Don't make your sentences too long. If you read your sentence aloud and you run out of breath before you get to the end of it, your sentence is too long.

Or you could be asthmatic. I hope you get medical help if you need it.

2. Items in a series should have parallel construction.
   Correct: I went to the store for apples, pears, and nuts.
   Incorrect: I went to the store for apples, pears, and ran into a friend.
3. Use active voice as much as possible. It's much more interesting than passive voice.
   Example of active voice: Linda grabbed the ketchup bottle.
   Example of passive voice: The ketchup bottle was grabbed.
   It's not that you can't use passive voice, but you should know what you're doing when you use it. Use it deliberately.
4. If a sentence works without a word, cut it.
   Example: Linda mistakenly thought that the woman handing her the ketchup bottle was just being nice.
   Better: Linda mistakenly thought the woman handing her the ketchup bottle was being nice.
5. A great main character is important, but don't forget secondary and bit characters such as the main character's best friend or the barista they get their coffee from every morning.
6. Address as many senses as possible. What does your main character see, smell, hear, taste, and feel?
7. It's very common to describe a main character's physical appearance with hair color and eye color. You can do better than that. Do they have any dimples or scars? What's the story behind their scars? Whether a scar is from childhood chicken pox or a knife fight can say a lot about a character. Are their clothes rough or soft, expensive or cheap? Do they have a soft belly for another character to rest their head? Or do they have hard muscles that make another character drool? Do they walk as if their feet don't touch the ground or does every footstep land like concrete?

8. Your characters should be different from each other. It's very easy to fall into the trap of making every character like yourself, but you should resist the urge. Spend some time getting to know your characters as individuals. Let that show through on the page.

9. Identify your personal writing foibles. For example, I also overuse the word "also." Also, since I'm a former newspaper reporter, I tend to have too many "she said" and "he said." I also have to remind myself that I'm telling a story, not reporting the news. Big difference.

10. If something is not important for plot or character development, cut it. You may have written a beautiful paragraph about how ketchup tastes, smells, feels, and looks, but if that has nothing to do with the story, cut it.

> *"Murder your darlings."—Sir Arthur*
> *Quiller-Couch*

A note about the 90% point: The closer you get to the end of your book, the louder the inner voice that tells you your writing is not good enough and "who do you think you are, thinking you could write a book?" may become. For me, that voice gets particularly loud when I am 90% done writing a book, which is why I refer to it as the "90% point." Your inner voice may be someone different, but for me it is my inner child trying to protect me from what can be a very harsh world. I give her a cookie and say some soothing words. I promise to protect her. That usually quiets her. Your inner voice may need other strategies, but you can get through this. I know it.

I've also recently learned that for some people, that voice is particularly loud at the 10% point, and it prevents them from getting very far or even starting a project. Do what you need to do to get past it and write your book.

A quick note about legal considerations: I'm not a lawyer, and laws vary around the world. Generally speaking, don't libel anyone. This means writing something wrong about someone that makes them look bad. Don't do it. Look, I know your ex did you wrong, but if you're going to write something nasty about them, be subtle. There's also the question of using brand names or the names of living famous people. You can, but you can't libel them either or make it look like they endorse you.

Aligning your writing with your goals

So, what should you write? The answer to this question depends on your goals. My goals are to write and publish the stories I want to read, make some money, and have a better life. That means that the lesbian fiction I write includes cozy paranormal mystery stories, sweet romance (all action stops at the bedroom door), romantic comedy, erotic romance (reader gets to see into the bedroom and more), and science fiction. Other popular sub-genres within lesbian fiction include thrillers, fantasy, young adult, new adult, children's books, detective novels, literary fiction, slow-burn romances, ice queen romances, age gap romances, historical romances, and much more.

It's a myth that only erotica is self-published. All genres are increasingly self-published.

If you just want to write something you love, do it. Pick a genre and do it. No other lesbian fiction in that genre? Even better, you must write it. Your goals can also change from project to project. When my mother-in-law was dying, I didn't have enough focus to write, but I did need something to do that could hold my attention. I ended up creating what is referred to as a "low-content book." These are books with minimal text such as journals with writing prompts, datebooks, coloring books, etc. Under another pen name, I spent the week creating and publishing a journal filled with quotes and writing prompts around the theme of connecting with your real self. That book sold next to nothing, although my best friend loved it. My brother quite liked it. It also kept me sane for a week. I regard that book as a success. I won't be addressing low-content books very much in this book, which is mostly focused on publishing fiction. I will mention them periodically, and there are some people who have found financial success with them.

If making a full-time living is a higher priority, you may need to use the write to market model outlined by Chris Fox (I'm a fan of this self-published author; all of his books are good). This means finding a balance between what you want to write and identifying market niches with underserved readers. For example, are there large numbers of readers looking for paranormal romance involving lesbian angels but not enough writers writing those books? Is the market for lesbian historical romance set in Regency times already flooded, and readers are drowning in choices?

Sales are never guaranteed in any genre, even if you do everything perfectly. However, writing in an underserved genre may increase your sales. You can identify these underserved niches by paying attention to the various bestseller lists on Amazon or accessing data on K-lytics. There is a charge to access their data, but it is good data. There are also several other companies that have various tools to scrape data from Amazon and other vendors to identify trends.

Ultimately, you should always feel good about your goals. I see writers moaning all the time, "When am I going to make it?" but they haven't defined what that means. You can't achieve a goal if you don't know what that goal is. It's like running a race without knowing how long the course is. I recommend using the SMART framework which stands for Specific, Measurable, Attainable (or Achievable), Relevant (or Realistic), and Time-bound.

An example from my life, regarding *My Favorite Wife*, a book I published in May 2023: my goals were to have the book published by the end of 2023 and have the book pay for itself.

Having the book pay for itself means that it pays for all of its cash outlays needed to get it published. In this case, this meant paying for the stock art used in the cover or about $3. I did everything else to publish that book myself or by trading skills with a friend.

See, I told you that publishing wasn't that expensive.

Anyway, that goal is Specific, Measurable, Attainable (or Achievable), Relevant (or Realistic), and Time-bound because the goal was to get the book published in a set amount of time and earn at least $3. It's specific. It's measurable in both time and money. It's attainable, which means it's less likely to stress me out. It's relevant to me and realistic.

Your goals should not stress you out, and that book has sold hundreds of copies.

How long should your book be?

How long a book should be depends on several factors. The nice thing about e-books is that length doesn't matter. I've published several 6,000-word short stories that sell very well. For print books, 24 pages is about as short as they can be. Forty thousand words is the minimum for a book to be considered a novel. It also depends on genre. Fantasy books often top 100,000 words because they require so much world building. A 200-page print book is about 60,000 words. Novelettes are defined as 10,000 to 17,500 words. Novellas are 17,500 to 40,000 words. Romance tends to be on the shorter side, but lots of long romance books exist. The story you have to tell should dictate the length. However, especially if you are writing to market, the length should be determined by the standards of your chosen genre.

Whatever you do, pick something, write it, and finish your first draft, because there is more fun to come.

CHAPTER FOUR

The 9 mistakes every beginner writer makes

1. Not Writing.
2. Not writing until you have created the perfect writing nook/space to write.

   I have a dedicated writing space. Only writing happens in that space, but I do write elsewhere. You are only allowed your own dedicated writing space if it doesn't stop you from writing elsewhere as needed.
3. Not writing until you can set aside the perfect dedicated two- or three-hour time slot and commit to doing so every day.

   Write every day. Don't write every day. Write for five minutes. Write for fifty minutes. Just write. Don't let the perfect get in the way of the good. Aim for progress not perfection.
4. Not writing until the book is perfectly plotted and outlined down to the last detail.

   There are plotters and pantsers in this world, and most healthy writers fall somewhere along this continuum. Write. Plot. Write. Plot. Vary the order. If you hit a wall while writing, you should do some plotting. If you hit a wall while plotting, you should do some writing.

5. Not writing because you're rewriting that one paragraph you already wrote over and over and over again.

Move on. Let it go. Come back to it later. Or never come back to it at all. Keep going.

6. Not writing because you'll only write if you can write something perfect the first time.

Even your published work won't be perfect. Write. Then write another draft. Maybe write another draft. Edit. Revise. Publish. Let it go.

7. Not writing because you think your ideas are stupid.

Your ideas are great. Any doubts? Read that sentence again. Read it aloud. Read it until it sinks in.

8. Not writing because you think your idea has been done before.

All ideas have been done before. Most stories are a version of "a stranger comes to town." There is no such thing as a truly original idea.

9. Not writing because you're creating the perfect marketing plan for a book that doesn't exist yet.

Marketing changes all the time. By the time you finish your book, your marketing plan will be useless and out of date. Don't waste your time. Besides, what's the point of having a marketing plan if you've nothing to market?

CHAPTER FIVE

Editing and revising

Revise, revise, revise

You've identified what you want to write. You have a great idea. You've written your first draft. Now what?

After completing the first draft of your novel, the next step is to revise and edit the manuscript. This involves going through the entire draft, reviewing the content, structure, and language used in the story. The goal is to refine and improve the work until it reaches a polished and coherent state.

This process will vary. I'm going to tell you my process for taking a first draft and turning it into a polished manuscript. Use this process or develop your own.

First, I take a break. For me, this means some chocolate and a short walk. I then read someone else's book or write something completely different like flash fiction in a genre I don't usually write in. Flash fiction is extremely short fiction ranging in length from 300-1,500 words.

Then, I write the second draft. This involves expanding descriptions and developing the secondary characters. I look for inconsistencies. If my main character starts out the book as a brunette vegan who likes to ice skate, she needs to end the book that way unless the story is about her dying her hair, starting to eat meat, and breaking a leg on the ice and never coming back. I look for opportunities to increase the drama and expand the plot. Could I give my bit characters more to do? Can the barista who serves the main character coffee every day also give sage advice? Maybe she should give bad advice that the main character has to learn the hard way to ignore? How is the pacing? Is it slow for 90 pages and then has an info dump in the last 10 pages? My characters don't have to be likable, but they do have to be people with whom I'd like to spend some time. Are they dull? What makes them interesting? Is my language clear? Am I using the correct forms of "your," "you're," "their," "they're," and "there"? Do my characters deserve their fate or am I being unnecessarily mean to them? Are there scenes that, while beautifully written, don't move the plot or develop the character and need to be cut?

When the second draft is finished, I take another break. This involves more chocolate, another walk, a swim, a glass of wine, and a nice present for myself because I deserve it. Now, it's time for the third draft. This involves a lot of the same steps as the second draft, but I'm working with a much more developed manuscript. It's really taking shape.

When the third draft is finished, I read it aloud, either to myself or to a friend. It's amazing how many things you can catch in this process, such as missed words and clunky sentences. If you trip over a sentence reading it aloud, then your readers will trip over it reading it to themselves. Change it. Make it better. If you don't have a buddy who will read with you, you can use built in AI audio tools. I find the voice for the AI audio in Microsoft Word too robotic, but there are lots of other options available.

The revision and editing process is a critical part of the

writing process, and taking the time to refine your work will help you create a more polished and successful novel.

All about editing

And now it's time to let your book go and either send it to an editor or begin the self-editing process.

Self-editing is possible and can create some good books, but I advise you to be realistic about your skills. Are you sure you can edit your own book? If you can, go for it.

Some self-editing tips:

1. **Take a break.** Before starting the editing process, take some time away from your manuscript. This helps you come back to the work with fresh eyes.
2. **Review the big picture.** Start by evaluating the overall story structure, plot, and character development. Make sure the story flows logically and your characters are well-rounded and consistent.
3. **Check for consistency.** Look for inconsistencies in plot, setting, and character traits. Make sure there are no contradictions or plot holes.
4. **Use strong language.** Make sure your language is clear, concise, and engaging. Use strong verbs and avoid unnecessary adverbs and adjectives. Is your character walking slowly or are they strolling? You can use adverbs and adjectives, but don't go overboard in using them or eliminating them.
5. **Cut the fluff.** Eliminate any unnecessary or repetitive language, including cliches or overused phrases. Is your character at the tipping point? Have they discovered a new normal? No. Just no.
6. **Proofread carefully.** Carefully proofread the manuscript for errors in grammar, punctuation, and spelling. Consider reading the manuscript backwards.

If you are unsure of your self-editing skills, get an editor. There are loads of professional editors who are worth the money they charge. There are loads who aren't. Always ask for a sample before committing to working with someone. Remember self-publishing means you are in charge. No one is doing you a favor by working for you. You are hiring someone. Take it seriously. Read whatever contract they ask you to sign. If they demand credit in the book listing or on the cover, run. That is not appropriate, although it is okay to include them in the front matter.

Also, make sure you know what you're getting. Here are the different types of editing:

1. **Developmental editing:** This type of editing focuses on the big picture of the manuscript, including plot, character development, pacing, and structure. The editor will work with you to refine and strengthen the overall story.
2. **Copy editing:** Copy editing is a more detailed type of editing that focuses on grammar, punctuation, spelling, and consistency. The editor will ensure the manuscript is free of errors and reads smoothly.
3. **Line editing:** Line editing is a type of editing that focuses on the finer details of the manuscript, such as sentence structure, word choice, and tone. The editor will work to improve the overall flow and style of the writing.
4. **Proofreading:** Proofreading is the final stage of editing and involves a careful review of the manuscript to catch any remaining errors or inconsistencies.

I recommend choosing an editor appropriate for your genre. I was once hired to edit some newspaper stories about cricket matches. I still don't understand the game, and while I made those stories grammatically correct, they probably would have turned out better with an editor who understood the game.

If you can't afford an editor, do not despair. Consider working with a trusted friend with skills in this area. I trade editing with a friend who is a literature professor at a university and has published dozens of books herself. She edits my writing. In exchange, I edit hers.

But seriously, let your book go. I know this is hard. This is like watching your first child going to their first day of school. You keep telling yourself you could make your book better. You worry about your child's, I mean book's, safety in someone else's hands, but here's the truth: at some point, you've done enough.

One of the most common questions I get asked is, "when do you know it's time? How do you know it's done?" Here's how:

1. The words no longer look like words. You've been working on it for so long that all you can see are rows of letters and spaces.
2. You start thinking of your main characters as your best friends, and you can't wait to hang out with them more. You can write a sequel with them, but, seriously, send them out into the world. You're done.
3. You've already obsessively culled all the stray adverbs and made the verbs so strong and precise that their next job will be plotting a spaceship's trajectory to Mars, complete with human cargo.
4. You've confirmed that you have used the correct forms of their, there, they're, your, and you're.
5. You start making changes that make things worse, not better.

Truthfully, no book is ever really done. Writers just move onto other projects. If William Shakespeare were still around, he'd be rewriting Macbeth—again! Let it go. Send your baby to that nice day care down the street.... I mean send your book to your editor and start working on something else.

When you get your manuscript back from your editor, don't take anything personally. Red marks, or whatever the digital equivalent is, are a sign of respect, although always remember it's your manuscript. You can disagree with your editor but, especially if you are paying them, are you getting your money's worth if all you do is discard their changes? It's all about balance. It's okay to disagree, but all of your editor's comments should lead to some questioning and deep thoughts that make your manuscript better. Remember, if you pay them, you're not paying them to stroke your ego. You're paying them to make your book better, and that is always possible.

Beta readers and sensitivity readers

After the final edit, it's time to send your book out to your beta readers. These lovely people are not editors, and they are not proofreaders. They are your product testers. In exchange for a free book, they agree to give you feedback. There are several Facebook groups devoted to linking authors and beta readers. I've seen people seek beta readers on Twitter and TikTok. I recruit my beta readers from my acquaintances, and I send these lovely people a formatted copy of my book and an optional worksheet that includes questions about how the story moves and their favorite characters. I give them a deadline of two to three weeks.

Once again, you don't have to do everything your beta readers suggest, but you should at least consider their suggestions. I also recommend recruiting more than one beta reader. I generally send my manuscripts to a half dozen friends, family, and acquaintances. About half of that number ends up sending me feedback, and that's okay. When considering the feedback, always consider the source. Are they your target readership? It's okay to get feedback from people who are not your intended audience, but context may dictate different actions than if they were. No matter what, be grateful for any and all feedback you receive.

Incorporate beta reader feedback as appropriate. It's okay to decide the feedback is not right for you or your work. It's okay to make changes that surprise yourself.

Should you use a sensitivity reader? Maybe. I'm a lesbian in an interracial same-sex marriage living in the Midwest. Many of my books are about interracial lesbian relationships.

I have used sensitivity readers when I have incorporated bisexual or trans characters into my work. These readers have been incredibly helpful because I don't include those characters to inadvertently hurt anybody. I include these characters because they reflect my world and people I respect. I want to get it right. Bringing in a sensitivity reader makes that more likely.

A note about cultural appropriation: Cultural appropriation is when someone from a dominant group uses an aspect of the culture of an oppressed community for financial gain when the oppressed community is prevented from doing so. It has been widely misinterpreted as meaning that people can only write about their own experiences. This is not true, but there are some key questions to consider as you write your story. Are you including diverse characters because it is an honest reflection of the world or are you writing someone else's experience? Is the story you are writing yours to tell? Are you using something sacred from one culture and disrespecting it or making light of it? Are you using someone else's culture as a costume? When in doubt, use a sensitivity reader. Consider paying them.

It is now time for the final proof, that one last read through. You should not be making any major changes at this point. Major changes increase the risk of a major error sneaking through. You should assume that there is at least one typo. You just have to find it. Hopefully, it's not in the title, and please don't misspell your own pen name.

Don't be scared. Your book is now ready to be published.

CHAPTER SIX

Formatting your book

You've written your book. You've revised it. You've had it edited and proofed. You've made it so good!

Now what?

A note about the 90% point that I mentioned in previous chapters: That inner voice that tells you your writing is not good enough and "Who do you think you are, thinking you can write a book?" may be getting particularly loud at this point. Don't fight that inner voice. Soothe it. Do something right now that rewards all your hard work. You just finished writing a book. You deserve a treat.

And now that you've given yourself a treat, onward.

It's time to publish. Doing it yourself means you don't have to wait for anyone's permission except your own. You don't need a publishing house. You don't need an agent. You don't even need that much, if any, money. The rise of the internet and the development of print-on-demand technology in the 1990s made it easier than ever for authors to self-publish their work. The emergence of e-readers and e-books in the early 2000s revolutionized book distribution and made it easier to sell your work.

"Nothing stinks like a pile of unpublished writing"—Sylvia Plath.

When I first started self-publishing in 2014, I published e-books on Kindle Direct Publishing/Amazon (KDP) and AllRomanceEbooks. I used Smashwords, a publishing aggregator, to distribute e-books to a wide range of other vendors such as Nook, Apple, and Kobo. I published paperbacks on CreateSpace.

AllRomanceEbooks shut down in 2016. KDP remains the behemoth in the U.S., although it's changed significantly over the years. CreateSpace was purchased by Amazon in 2005 and merged with KDP in 2020. Draft2Digital, another publishing aggregator, acquired Smashwords in 2022.

Things change all the time, and you have a lot more choices for publishing platforms. In this chapter I explore book formatting in a general way. In Chapters Twelve through Twenty, I get into the requirements and nuances of various platforms. Although the technical requirements for covers are included in Chapters Twelve through Twenty, the ins and outs of cover design are discussed in Chapter Seven.

A note about e-books versus print: I recommend not getting hung up on format. I know lots of people regard paper books fondly. I'm one of them, but e-books have a distribution that cannot be matched by print books. My e-books reach those for whom mail is unreliable and brick-and-mortar bookstores are non-existent or unable (legally) or unwilling to carry books about lesbians. I've sold print books in many countries. I've sold e-books in even more. I feel particularly proud when I sell a book, usually an e-book, in a country in which I am illegal.

This is why self-publishing rocks—especially for lesbians.

Formatting your book is the next step in the process.

This involves making sure the text is laid out correctly and formatted for the publishing platform you will be using. Ensure that you adhere to the platform's guidelines, so your book is properly displayed on all devices. Formatting for the various platforms has a lot of commonalities, so don't get scared. One version often needs only a few tweaks, if any, to be good to go for another platform. The differences are outlined in Chapters Twelve through Twenty.

Key points: When formatting an e-book, you want the text to flow. It will work whether it is converted to an EPUB (the most common virtual book format), a PDF, or any other virtual book format. It will be device agnostic. This means people are able to read your book on any device they happen to be using whether it is a dedicated e-reader, a smartphone, or a laptop computer. This is the opposite of paper. When creating a paper book, you want your text to be fixed on the page. You don't want it to move. You want it to look good and be readable exactly as it is.

Remember, in self-publishing the author is in charge, but that doesn't mean you have to do everything. You can hire a book formatter if need be. Also, while my process can be quite manual, and I like it that way, many self-publishers use various software to speed up the process.

Basics of e-book formatting

You can use software such as Vellum or Atticus if that works for you, but this is the process I use for creating a document that can be converted into an e-book. My initial document is created in Google Docs because I write with my wife. This allows us to share the document and work on it together at the same time. When the manuscript is finished, I download it to Microsoft Word. My advice going forward is focused on Word, but you can, of course, use other programs.

Note: I am a big fan of the Smashwords Style Guide. It

was one of the most useful books when I first started self-publishing, and it still is.

1. I turn off auto correct and auto format. In auto format, uncheck all boxes except curly quote marks. You want the nice curly quote marks.
2. I do a find and replace for single and double quote marks to make sure they are the nice curly quote marks.
3. I replace double paragraph returns with single paragraph returns. This involves searching for ^p^p and replacing them with ^p.
4. I select all and clear all formatting. On Microsoft Word that means I hit control-A (select all) and then select "clear" from the editing menu.
5. I then go through the document and use stylesheets to apply various formatting such as font size, font color, spacing, and alignment. I add italics and bold as appropriate.

Do not format text directly, except for making text bold or italic. That formatting will not stick once your manuscript is converted by the various platforms. Use style sheets.

How to use stylesheets in Microsoft Word: On the right-hand side of the home tab, there is a "styles pane." You can use the stylesheets that come with Microsoft Word or create your own. The font color for all style sheets should be set to "automatic," not black. This will allow various e-readers to convert your document to reader preferences. For example, some readers read on a black screen with white or otherwise light-colored text. If your stylesheet is set to black, that text will become unreadable. Be nice to your readers, especially those with visual impairments. Set your font color to automatic.

A note on accessibility: Another reason to love e-books is that a reader can adjust the settings on an e-reader to suit them, their comfort, and their abilities. This is not possible with paper books. As self-publishers we must make that process as easy as possible. That means setting the text color to "automatic" and, if you have any images in your book, make sure you include an "alt text" description for those who cannot see the image. This is good practice for readers who may have visual impairments as well as those around the world whose e-readers may struggle or not be able to handle graphics.

I insert front matter at the start of my book. This is centered on the page in 12-point Times New Roman font and includes:

- Title
- Series name and volume if it is part of a series
- Author name
- Publisher name (optional; you can come up with a company name for your self-publishing efforts, but you don't have to.)
- Statement of copyright with the year and the name of the owner of the copyright
- This text:
- Thank you for downloading this e-book. This book remains the copyrighted property of the author and may not be redistributed to others for commercial or non-commercial purposes. If you enjoyed this book, please encourage your friends to download their own copy from their favorite authorized retailer. Thank you for your support.

NO AI TRAINING: Without in any way limiting the author's exclusive rights under copyright, any use of this publication to "train" generative artificial intelligence (AI) technologies to generate text is expressly prohibited. The author reserves all rights to license uses of this work for generative AI training and development of machine learning language models.

All characters and events in this book are fictitious. Any resemblance to actual persons, living or dead, is strictly coincidental.

- A statement that says film and TV rights are available and a contact email address. No one has yet asked me for film and TV rights, but I have a dream. I'm ready for it to come true.
- A link to sign up for my email newsletter. This is optional, and email newsletters are discussed in Chapter Nine.
- A list of other titles (Optional. It's not just okay that this may be your first book. It's FABULOUS!). I like including a hotlink when possible. This is generally allowable in books uploaded directly to a vendor but not an aggregator. For example, you can include links to your books for sale on Amazon in the books you upload to Kindle Direct Publishing (KDP). If you upload directly to Kobo, you can include links to your other books for sale on Kobo. Smashwords/Draft2Digital, an aggregator, doesn't allow hotlinks because they distribute to a lot of vendors, and those vendors will not allow links to other sales platforms besides their own.
- My editor's name
- A thank you for my beta readers and others who contributed in some way to the book

The next page is a table of contents. Most vendors will accept a table of contents that is hotlinked to bookmarks within your document. To add a bookmark, put your cursor where you want it placed, go to Word's insert menu, and select "bookmark." Bookmarks must have a single word name, no spaces. Make sure the "hidden bookmarks" box is checked in the bookmark popup and delete any hidden bookmarks. They can randomly appear and may mess with your formatting. KDP is the main vendor that requests a table of contents in a different format, and I address that in Chapter Thirteen.

I then go through the manuscript and apply formatting using stylesheets such as chapter title, subhead, and main text or paragraph. For the main text, I like a 0.3-inch first line indent. **DO NOT USE TABS TO INDENT TEXT. DO NOT USE THE SPACE BAR TO INDENT TEXT.** Some authors prefer not to have an indent for the first paragraph of each chapter. For e-books, I'm not convinced it matters that much. The main text should be single spaced, 12 point, Times New Roman. Set font color to automatic. Do NOT use multiple paragraph returns to create a page break and move to the next page. Insert a page break from the "layout" or "insert" menus if you are using Word. I'm sure other programs have their own real page breaks.

I end my book with the symbols ###. I thank the reader and then tell them what I want them to do next. For some books, I want readers to go to the next book in the series. For others, I want them to sign up for my email newsletter.

It's okay if you have neither another book nor an email list. You can still thank your reader, and you can ask them to review your book on a vendor or on a reader site like Goodreads.

Should you include the first chapter of your next book if you have one? There's a lot of debate about this in the self-publishing community. It makes a lot of sense, but readers don't seem to like it. I don't do it. The choice is yours.

Basics of paper book formatting (paperbacks and hard covers)

While you want e-books to flow and look good on any device, you want paper books, whether printed as paperbacks or hardcovers, to be fixed on the page. That means that while the secret to a good e-book layout is understanding style sheets, the secret to good paper book layout is understanding section breaks.

Section breaks are used to separate different parts of a document, such as chapters or sections with different formatting. A section break creates a new section in the document, allowing you to apply different formatting, page numbers, headers, and footers to each section.

There are three types of section breaks in Microsoft Word:

1. Next page section break: This type of section break starts the new section on the next page. It's commonly used to start a new chapter.
2. Continuous section break: This type of section break starts the new section on the same page. It's useful for creating columns or formatting changes within a single page. I haven't used these for fiction books which tend to have fairly straightforward layouts, but I have used them for non-fiction books when I want a more creative layout.
3. Even page or odd page section break: This type of section break starts the new section on the next even or odd page. It's commonly used in books and other printed materials to ensure that chapters always start on the right- or left-hand side of the page.

To insert a section break in Microsoft Word, go to the Page Layout tab, click on "breaks," and select the type of section break you want to insert.

Now that you know how to use section breaks, you are ready to layout your paper book. KDP has templates that are a good start and that I recommend. Other print on demand paper book publishers have their own templates. I like 6"x9" trim size for fiction. Other self-published authors use 5"x8" or 5.5"x8.5". Like much in self–publishing, it's ultimately your decision, although I do suggest choosing a size and sticking to it. Readers tend to prefer that their paper books from one author are all the same size, so they look nice on a shelf.

I suggest laying out your paper book with one of your favorite books sitting next to you, so you can use it as a model. My books are usually formatted as follows:

The first page of your paper book should include in large type your book title and author. If the book is part of a series, include the series name and volume number.

The next page is the indicia, also known as the title page or the copyright page. I include the title, series name and volume number if it is part of a series, author name, a copyright statement, a statement about AI training, a statement that this book is fiction, an email address that people can use to contact me for film and TV rights, a list of other titles in my series, a list of my other books, the editor credit, more copyright information, an ISBN number, and my publisher logo.

You don't have to have a publisher name or logo if you don't want one. It's optional.

There is a lot of debate in the self-publishing community about where to get ISBNs (International Standard Book Numbers). Should you buy them? Should you use free ones from the various vendors? I always use the free ones from the various vendors, but many self-published authors buy them from Bowker, the official ISBN agency. Ultimately, it's your decision. I've never paid for an ISBN, and I don't regret that decision. If you do buy them, remember you need one for each edition. If you get a free ISBN from one vendor, you can't use that number on another vendor (e.g., you can't use a Smashwords/Draft2Digital ISBN on KDP).

On the next page, I put the title of the book, series name and volume number if there is one, author name, and the blurb. The page after that may be blank or include a dedication. The next page has the title, series name and volume number if there is one, and author name again. The table of contents comes next. Then it is time to start laying out the book. I like to put the chapter head about a quarter of the way down the first page of each chapter. The first paragraph is not indented. The rest of the paragraphs are.

At the end of the book, I include an "about the author" page with my bio and a QR code that will lead a reader to what I want them to do next, usually subscribe to my email newsletter. You can create a free QR code in Google Chrome or Canva. I then include a few pages of information about my other titles. If you don't have other titles or an email newsletter, you can always thank your reader, ask them to write a review, and write an author's note.

Basics of audiobook production

The audiobook market generated $1.6 billion in revenue in 2021, and this book format is more popular than ever. Publishing your lesbian fiction as an audiobook can attract a broader audience, including those who enjoy listening to books during their commute, workout sessions, or while engaging in other activities. It can increase the accessibility of your work and reach individuals who may not typically read physical or digital books.

Note: Books are books. E-books are real books. Paperbacks are real books. Hardbacks are real books. Audiobooks are real books, and here's what you need to know to make yours a reality. The specifics of the various audiobook platforms will be covered in Chapters Twelve through Twenty, and here are three ways to turn your manuscript into an audiobook.

Hire a narrator
Hiring and working with a narrator to create an audiobook involves several steps.

1. **Determine your audiobook budget:** Before you start searching for a narrator, establish your budget for the project. Narrator fees can vary based on factors such as experience, reputation, and the length of your book. Some narrators are paid outright. Others are open to royalty share arrangements. A talented friend or family member willing to give you a break can make audiobook production even less expensive.

2. **Find potential narrators:** Audiobook production platforms such as ACX (Audiobook Creation Exchange) and Findaway Voices have databases of narrators you can browse and contact. Various websites offer directories of voice actors and narrators that you can explore. Seek recommendations from other authors who have worked with narrators before.
3. **Review samples and demos:** Request samples or demos from potential narrators to assess their voice, style, and suitability for your book. Listen carefully to their pronunciation, pacing, tone, and ability to convey emotions.
4. **Conduct auditions or interviews:** Narrow down your list of potential narrators and conduct auditions or interviews to assess their compatibility with your book. You can ask them to read specific passages or conduct a short phone or video interview to discuss their approach and availability.
5. **Finalize the contract and terms:** Once you've chosen a narrator, discuss the terms of the project, including the fee, payment schedule, timeline, and any other relevant details. It's important to have a written agreement or contract that outlines these terms to avoid misunderstandings later on.
6. **Provide guidance and materials:** Share your manuscript and any specific instructions or guidelines with the narrator. Provide character descriptions, pronunciation guides for names or unusual words, and any notes regarding the tone or style you envision for the narration.
7. **Collaboration and communication:** Maintain open and frequent communication with the narrator throughout the production process. Address any questions or concerns they may have and provide feedback on their initial recordings or samples. Collaboration and mutual understanding are key to achieving the desired audiobook result.

8. **Review and provide feedback:** As the narrator completes chapters or sections, review their recordings and provide feedback on areas that may need adjustments or revisions. Maintain a constructive and professional approach to ensure a productive working relationship.
9. **Finalize the production:** Once all the recordings are completed, work with the narrator to address any revisions or edits. Ensure that the audio files meet the technical specifications required by your chosen audiobook distribution platform.

Narrate the book yourself

Do you have a good voice? Maybe you'd like to narrate your own book, which is more common than you might think. Stephen King, Maya Angelou, Prince Harry (Duke of Sussex), Barbara Kingsolver, Toni Morrison, David Sedaris, and many other authors narrate their own books. There's no reason you can't. You will need to:

1. **Prepare your recording space:** Find a quiet and controlled environment for recording. Choose a room with minimal background noise and good acoustics. Believe it or not, the best place in your house to record an audiobook is probably your coat closet. The coats act like sound proofing and can reduce echo, which is why my wife and I are in the process of building one in our coat closet. Consider putting a do-not-disturb sign on the door to prevent the people you live with from interrupting your recording. You can also rent a recording space if you don't have a good place in your home. It takes about four hours to record 10,000 words of text, so when renting space take the length of your work into account when booking the time.
2. **Purchase a good-quality microphone, headphones, and a pop filter to reduce sounds:** A USB microphone or a condenser microphone with an audio

interface can provide professional-grade sound. Use headphones to monitor the audio while recording.

3. **Set up recording software:** Install audio recording software on your computer. Popular options include Audacity (free and open source), Adobe Audition, or GarageBand (for Mac users). Familiarize yourself with the software and its features.

4. **Practice vocal techniques:** Before recording, practice vocal techniques such as breathing control, articulation, and pacing. Warm up your voice with vocal exercises to ensure clarity and consistency throughout the narration.

5. **Plan your recording sessions:** Create a schedule for recording sessions to maintain consistency and manage your time effectively. Consider your voice's endurance and set realistic targets for each session.

6. **Create a recording script:** Prepare a script that includes your book's text, including any stage directions, character descriptions, or other important notes. Break down the script into manageable sections or chapters to facilitate recording.

7. **Record your narration:** Start recording chapter by chapter or section by section. Maintain a consistent microphone distance and speak clearly and naturally. Take breaks between sections to rest your voice and maintain vocal quality.

8. **Monitor and edit your recordings:** Listen to each recording carefully and identify any mistakes, background noises, or inconsistencies. Use audio editing software to remove unwanted sections, correct errors, and ensure a smooth and professional-sounding narration.

9. **Edit and enhance the audio:** Apply audio editing techniques to improve the overall sound quality. Adjust volume levels, equalization, and dynamics to ensure a balanced and pleasing listening experience.

10. **Review and revise your narration:** Once the initial editing is complete, listen to the entire audiobook and

review it for any further revisions or improvements. Pay attention to pacing, tone, and overall performance. Make necessary adjustments to achieve the desired result.

11. **Export the final audio files:** Export the edited and finalized audio files to a suitable format, such as WAV or MP3, ensuring compatibility with your chosen audiobook distribution platform's requirements (described in Chapters Twelve through Twenty). Each chapter should have its own audio file.

AI narration

Using AI for anything is controversial. I'm not trying to put anyone out of business, but AI narration utilizing a computer-generated synthesized voice is a possibility. Several platforms either allow AI recordings or provide the technology to create these recordings.

I have created a handful of AI-narrated audiobooks. Some things to be aware of when using AI narration:

1. AI narrators sound very human, but they can't emote. They can't act. I've written several gay male erotic romances that I have transformed into audiobooks using AI. They sound like Morgan Freeman reading gay porn.
2. You still need to spend time reviewing the recordings and correcting any mispronunciations.
3. They take less time than creating human-narrated audiobooks, but they still take time.

I do like AI-narrated audiobooks, but I don't view them as an endpoint. I view them as a stepping stone to creating human-narrated audiobooks. I used to find the idea of creating audiobooks daunting. I learned a lot creating AI-narrated audiobooks and look forward to taking what I learned and creating human-narrated audiobooks.

Now that you know the basics of e-book, paperback, hardcover, and audiobook formatting and production, I'll get into the specific requirements of various publishing platforms in Chapters Twelve through Twenty. Always remember, you don't have to do everything. It's better to be happy and proud of what you have achieved than to stretch yourself too thin physically or financially. Burnout is never worth it.

Now it is time to make a cover for your fabulous book.

CHAPTER SEVEN

Cover design

The saying "don't judge a book by its cover" is a great metaphor for life and interacting with people. It's terrible advice for self-published authors. Readers judge books by their covers all the time. They may say they don't, but they are lying.

The cover of your book is the first thing that readers see, and it is essential to make it eye-catching and visually appealing if you want people to read what's inside. Keep in mind that the cover should accurately represent the content of your book while also standing out in a crowded market. Most importantly, the cover must reflect your genre. You can create your own cover or hire a designer to create one for you. A cover can be expensive, but it doesn't have to be. Remember, publishing work should pay for publishing activities. Don't go into debt to publish your book.

In this chapter, I explore the various strategies for making a cover and then get into what should go on a cover. In Chapters Twelve through Twenty I discuss the cover requirements of the various self-publishing platforms.

Working with a designer

Working with a professional designer is a good idea if your graphic design skills are not that strong, you don't want to learn graphic design, or you don't want to design your own cover. It's a myth that self-published authors do everything themselves. Self-publishing puts the author in charge, but it's important to hire when necessary. You don't have to do everything. Your time is valuable. Use it judiciously.

The first step is to determine your budget. Cover design costs vary widely, so you'll want to make sure you have a clear idea of how much you're willing and able to pay. While hiring a professional cover designer can be expensive, there are many who offer more affordable rates. I recommend asking other self-published authors on social media for recommendations. If you see a cover you like on a book, contact the author or publisher for a recommendation. There are several online marketplaces, but I haven't used those platforms. I recommend May Dawney who designs many covers of lesbian books, including several of mine. Her prices are reasonable, and her work is excellent. (https://maydawneydesigns.com/)

After you have identified a potential designer, your next step is to review their portfolio. Look for designers who have experience designing covers in your genre. Specificity matters. If they understand cover design for lesbian romance, do they understand the aesthetics of lesbian science fiction?

You can then contact the designer to introduce yourself and provide information about your book. Include the genre, the tone of the book, and any key themes or symbols that you would like to see incorporated into the cover. Try to identify one salient selling point to highlight. What are you really selling? I write, publish, and sell a lot of romance fiction, but what I'm really selling is relaxation. My covers reflect that. Discuss and agree on timelines, deliverables, and payment terms. Get as much in writing as possible. If they give you a contract to sign, read it. As the designer creates drafts of the cover, provide feedback on what you like and don't like. Be specific about any changes you want to see but be open to the designer's suggestions. The process should be as collaborative as possible. Once you're happy with the design, finalize the cover and make any final payments to the designer.

Remember, the cover of your book is the first thing readers will see, so take your time and choose a cover designer who can create a design that will attract readers and accurately reflect the tone and genre of your book. There are several common mistakes that self-published authors make when working with a cover designer. I asked May Dawney about her experiences. These are her recommendations for self-published authors:

1. **Do your own research first but trust in the skill of your designer.** A lot of first-time authors come to me either with a completely rigid idea or zero idea at all. The first tends to lead to a cover that we call being "designed-by-proxy," which tends to be off-genre and usually does not appeal to the target audience. The latter leads to a lot of floundering and (expensive) editing rounds. For us as designers, the middle is where we love to be: the author has done their own research, they know what their competition uses for a cover and what's on trend, but they are not hung up on a single idea, leaving us room to work our magic.

2. **Provide a complete brief.** We get that it's hard to know what to share with us to get the best result. That's why designers have a form to fill in, or we have a chat about your book before we start. But if your main character has pink hair or you have this one book cover in mind as a style inspiration, it's important you share that information before your designer gets going. I know a cover can seem expensive, but we spend

many hours on our designs, and we have a lot of costs. Every edit round that can be avoided is a kindness to your designer, even if it's included in your package, especially when the change is so incredibly obvious.

3. **Know what your book is about, which genre(s) it is, and which categories you'll be putting your book in on Amazon or other book selling platforms.** Have an elevator pitch ready for us so we have a good starting point. "My book is an urban fantasy WLW first-in-series. It's about 18-year-old fire mage Cassie and her best friend Raine, a spirit caller, who fight underworld creatures in a fictional city in the U.S., which I based loosely on Chicago." From there on, we can ask more questions, but we have all we need to form a good idea of what you will need to reach your target audience.

Buying a pre-made cover

Premade book covers are a popular option for self-published authors who are looking for a professional cover design on a tight budget or timeline. You can scour premade book cover marketplaces online for something that works with your manuscript, and many designers, including May Dawney, have a selection of premades.

Additionally, this may sound counter intuitive, but while often the manuscript comes first and the cover is created to suit, sometimes the cover comes first. It is not uncommon for authors to buy a premade cover and then write a manuscript that fits it, and there is nothing wrong with that. (I've always imagined a world where creative professionals are in charge. You can have a situation with an author in charge and editors and cover designers working for them, or you can have a cover designer or editor in charge with other creatives working for them and all sorts of other variations. But I digress.)

Things to keep in mind when considering premade book covers:

1. **Be sure to confirm what rights you are buying to the cover and the images included in it.** Can you use it on an e-book? A paperback? What if you decide to put it on a t-shirt? What if you decide to sell that t-shirt?

2. **They may not perfectly fit your book.** While premade covers can be a great option for authors who are in a rush or on a budget, it's important to keep in mind that the cover may not perfectly match the tone or content of your book. You may need to be flexible with your expectations and willing to compromise on some aspects of the design. You may need to make some tweaks to your book to better match the cover.

3. **You may need to spend a lot of time finding one that is good for your book,** and you may not be able to find something that perfectly matches your needs.

4. **You should still do your research.** Just because a cover is premade doesn't mean it's automatically a good fit for your book. Make sure you do your research and find a cover that accurately reflects your book's tone and genre and that will appeal to your target audience.

Designing your own

One of the more pleasant surprises for me from self-publishing over the past decade is that I have been able to learn, and grow to love, book cover design. It may not be for you. That's okay. Not everything is for everybody, but, if you would like to give it a try, go for it.

Here is my cover design story.

When I started self-publishing, I was also publishing some books with a small e-book-first publisher. For my first self-published books, I used that publisher's designer. When that designer decided to wind down her cover design business, I made the decision to design my own covers. I had experience laying out magazines, and I wanted to see if I would enjoy book cover design before we started hunting for a new designer. I also wanted to see if I could be any good at it.

Remember, graphic design is a skill like writing. Respect it. Respect what it takes to be good at it.

I started out on Canva, which has both a website and a phone app. They have a fairly generous free level, and images, fonts, and templates can be inexpensive. Also, very important, they have free design courses. It's not enough to understand the software. You need to understand design principles as well.

I then moved on to Pixlr, also free. I'm currently using Adobe Photoshop, which costs me about $11 a month. I buy stock photos from Depositphotos. Most stock photo libraries offer subscriptions. It can be very challenging to buy just one stock photo. About three times a year, you can get a 100-photo package at a deep discount for Depositphotos that doesn't expire from AppSumo. I studied book covers. I analyzed what worked and what didn't. I took some graphic design classes from Canva, Udemy, and Adobe to make it more likely that my covers rocked.

In addition to Depositphotos, I periodically download and use images from free open access photo libraries such as UnSplash and Pixabay. Other public domain libraries include:

1. Wikimedia Commons: Wikimedia Commons is a massive database of over 25 million freely usable media files, including images, videos, and sound clips. The platform is a project of the Wikimedia Foundation and contains works that are in the public domain or licensed under Creative Commons licenses.
2. New York Public Library Digital Collections: The New York Public Library's Digital Collections feature over 700,000 images that are free to use and share. The

images include prints, photographs, maps, and more, and cover a wide range of subjects.

3. Library of Congress Prints & Photographs Online Catalog: The Library of Congress Prints & Photographs Online Catalog contains over 1 million digitized images from the library's collections. The images are free to use and cover a wide range of subjects, from historical events to portraits to landscapes.

4. Public Health Image Library. This is run by the Centers for Disease Control and Prevention and provides thousands of current and historic images related to global public health.

Make sure you read the terms and conditions before you use a photo. There are two main things to consider.

1. **Photographer's copyright.** The person who took the photo owns the copyright to the photo unless there is a contract saying otherwise. Do not violate someone's copyright.

2. **Right of publicity.** Any identifiable people in the photo have the right of publicity. This means you need to make sure a model release is on file. Paid stock photo libraries will always have a model release on file. This is unlikely to be true for free photo libraries. You should be careful associating an individual with something that could be embarrassing or making it look like someone famous is endorsing your book when they haven't. My general rule of thumb is to not use photos from public domain libraries that have identifiable people in them. That model release is important. You also want to avoid any photos with identifiable brands or copyrighted characters. Unsplash has some photos that include toys from Star Wars. I would not put those photos on one of my book covers. **WHATEVER YOU DO, DO NOT, I REPEAT, DO NOT DOWNLOAD RANDOM IMAGES FROM**

THE INTERNET AND TAKE THEM FOR YOUR COVERS. THIS IS THEFT FROM BOTH THE PHOTOGRAPHER AND THE MODEL. JUST BECAUSE A PHOTO IS PUBLICLY AVAILABLE DOES NOT MEAN IT'S IN THE PUBLIC DOMAIN. IF IT HAS A WATERMARK FROM A STOCK PHOTO LIBRARY, A PHOTOGRAPHER, OR AN ARTIST, YOU CANNOT USE IT WITHOUT GETTING A LICENSE TO DO SO. USING SOFTWARE TO REMOVE SOMEONE ELSE'S WATERMARK WHEN YOU HAVEN'T PAID FOR THE IMAGE IS THEFT.

Some examples of the consequences for violating other people's copyright and not following the terms of service of stock photo libraries and publishing platforms:

1. Various publishing platforms can shut down your account with little or no warning and keep whatever royalties you've earned thus far.
2. You can be sued. Think you're too small? No one will notice? In December 2020, the U.S. passed a law called Copyright Alternative in Small-Claims Enforcement Act of 2020 (CASE Act) effectively setting up a copyright small claims process. Don't violate copyright. You will get caught.

When I was working for a small magazine in the 1990s, I profiled a celebrity, expecting him never to see the article I wrote about him without interviewing him. I did my research. I interviewed other people who knew him. That lawsuit didn't cost me or my magazine a lot of money in the end, but it could have bankrupted us. Also, it was not fun. Don't do anything on the expectation, "Oh, they'll never see it."

About AI generated art and covers: AI generated artwork cannot be copyrighted, and there are several lawsuits pending because AI generated artwork uses the copyrighted artwork and photography of human artists and photographers. Maybe you could use it for some inspiration, but at the moment I'm not willing to recommend that you publish with AI art on your cover. If you do use AI generated art, make sure you follow the terms of service of the platform that generated it.

What should go on your cover?

I've listed several strategies for getting a good cover, but what should you put on your cover? A cover should include the title and your pen name. If it's part of a series, include the series title and the volume number. Do NOT include pricing or temporary promotional offers. Do not put a # before any numbers. Don't put "by" before your pen name. Some covers include endorsements, reviews, or awards.

Remember: Those digital images on online book sellers can be pretty small. You want it to look attractive when it is full size, but also as a thumbnail.

The image should be determined by the subgenre of lesbian fiction in which you are writing. Illustrated covers are increasingly popular. Some lesbian readers really don't like people on their book covers. Others love them. I recommend looking at the Amazon top ten list for lesbian fiction for suggestions as to what is currently popular.

The biggest mistake I see in book covers is too much going on, too many objects, settings, and people. Pick one. Okay, maybe two. Keep it simple: A minimalist design can be just as effective as a more complex one, and it's often easier and cheaper to create. Stick to a simple color palette, use clear fonts, and incorporate one or two key elements that represent your book's genre or theme.

Choose a font that reflects your genre, and don't use too many of them. For example, script fonts are popular for romance. Thick serif fonts are more popular for military stories. Don't put the title on the very edge of the book cover. Don't be afraid to put it in the center over the image and use design techniques to ensure it is readable.

A note about designing covers that can be seen in public: For e-books, a cover cannot be easily seen by others nearby. This is not true for paperbacks or hard covers. A reader may not want to be seen reading a book with a racy cover in public. This may be particularly true if your novel is intended to be read by teens. Most books do just fine with one cover, but you may want to consider two covers, one for the e-book and one for the paperback, depending on the book itself and the target market. One of the many advantages of e-books is that people around you can't see what you're reading. This has been one of the explanations for the popularity of the book *50 Shades of Grey*. However, my dirtiest book, *Give Me Thorns*, is also my biggest seller as a paperback. So, as noted previously, conventional wisdom is not always useful.

As part of the research for this book I asked the members of the Facebook group Sapphic Book Lovers, a group of about 11,000 readers, their biggest pet peeves about the covers of sapphic books.

Many really hated covers with photos of people who didn't look like the characters in the book. Stock photo libraries don't have a lot of lesbian images, especially for queers of color, so this is most likely a reflection of limited resources.

Some didn't like stock photos of people who didn't seem queer. Tough call because queers can look like anyone. Getting your own photos taken can get expensive, but there are other options including illustrated or abstract covers.

Others didn't like illustrated or cartoon-like covers, but some loved them. Quite a few didn't like people on the covers, while others liked them. Several didn't like sexy covers, although those are appropriate for lesbian erotica or erotic romance.

So, what should you do?

Sir Alec Issigonis, designer of the original Mini car in 1959, said, "A camel is a horse designed by committee." The Mini became one of the most successful cars of all time. Sir

Alec was knighted in 1969 because of its success. The car was voted the second most influential car of the 20th century.

When asked about customer input in the development of the Ford Model T, Henry Ford said, "If I had asked people what they wanted, they would have said faster horses."

So, really, what should you do?

Try to fit your genre, but ultimately, it's your book. It's your decision. Also remember that you can always produce a second edition with an even better cover.

CHAPTER EIGHT

Mastering pull marketing

*"Writing is about you. Publishing is about
the book. Marketing is about the reader."—
Successful Self-Publishing by Joanna Penn*

The number one question I get asked when I tell people about my writing and self-publishing is about how I market my books. How do I alert readers to their existence? Great question. I'm never sure what to say because the answer is both simple and complicated. In this chapter, I'm going to explore the principles of pull marketing and then get into the details. Other types of marketing are covered in Chapters Nine, Ten, and Eleven. Publishing platforms often have built in dedicated marketing tools, and I will explore those in Chapters Twelve through Twenty.

Most writers say they hate marketing, but I believe that's mostly because they don't really understand what marketing is. It doesn't have to entail nagging an endless list of bloggers to review your book (and honestly most of them probably wish you would stop) or hawking your book to friends, family, and anyone who will listen. If you do, you may find yourself getting fewer invites to parties because they wish you would stop too. Marketing does start the minute you put words on the page, and it doesn't have to be scary or awful.

Pull marketing versus push marketing: Most people, when they think about marketing, think about all the times they see advertisements or other calls to buy, buy, buy. That is the tip of the iceberg when it comes to marketing. It's important to know the difference between "pull" marketing and "push" marketing. Pull marketing, also known as passive marketing and discussed in this chapter, occurs when someone goes to a bookstore (brick-and-mortar or online) and starts searching for something to read. They type in search terms or ask a store clerk, and they pull a book toward them. This is the most important part of marketing and leads to 80% of my sales. Push marketing, discussed in Chapter Nine, is when a publisher (you) advertises or posts on social media, "buy this" or "buy that." A book is being pushed toward a reader who will hopefully buy it.

Note: There are a million things you can do to market your book. You don't have to do everything. You should probably keep your marketing list short. It's better to do one marketing strategy very well than to do ten poorly. Don't let anyone tell you that you **MUST** do one thing or another, especially if they've never even written a book, let alone published one. Do what makes you comfortable. If you are comfortable on Facebook and your readers are there, stay there. If you enjoy making TikTok videos, continue having fun there. If you hate both of those platforms, don't feel like you have to join them.

Marketing is like exercise. The best one is the one you will actually do.

Also note: While I encourage you to do what you are comfortable with, I also encourage you to push beyond your comfort zone. You may surprise yourself with what you end up enjoying.

Or not. It's okay to try something and have it not work out.

And another note: Marketing is the aspect of self-publishing that is subject to the most change. The things I did a decade ago to market my books are no longer useful, and the things I do now didn't even exist.

And this is why you don't write your marketing plan before you write your book. The marketing plan will be out of date long before your book is ever finished.

One more thing: Most of the time you won't know why you sold a book. Don't drive yourself crazy. Let it go. There are some things you are just never going to understand.

Anyway, this is as good a time as any to reflect on the goals you hopefully developed in Chapter Three. Whatever marketing you do should be in alignment with your goals—not anyone else's. Your goals can change, but they should always be yours and yours alone.

Onward. Let's get into pull marketing, which is the best. I love it. I mean, who wouldn't? It means that you put something good out there. People look for it. They find it. They pull it toward them. They buy it. What's not to love?

Pull marketing is the most important part of your marketing strategy. Do not neglect it. It involves writing a good book, getting a good edit, laying out the book well, getting a good cover, categorizing your book properly, and developing good keywords.

I bet there were some things on that list that surprised you, like the fact that writing a good book is the first and most important step in a marketing plan. Without that, the rest of your marketing plan is of limited usefulness. You can have the best marketing plan that money can buy, but if you're attempting to sell a poorly written book that no one wants to read it can only do so much.

If you are writing to market, write a book that fits the specific niche you are aiming for. Some good books sell. Some don't. Some bad books sell, but they are less likely to sell than good books. Refer back to Chapter Three to learn how to write a good book and about writing to market.

Creating metadata

Your next step is to write great metadata. This will allow pull marketing to really work some magic. Metadata, data about data, allows readers to find your books.

The first piece of metadata is your title. What should you call your book? The title should be attention-grabbing, evocative, and reflective of the themes and tone of the story. You're looking for one to five words, the fewer the better, that capture your book's essence. You can look at best-selling lesbian books in your sub-genre for inspiration. It's okay to use the same title as a book that is already published. Titles are not copyrightable, but I would avoid any situation that creates confusion. If your book title and cover design are too similar to a book already on the market, you could disappoint and frustrate readers looking for a different book. For example, there are several books on the market called "Her," but they have different subtitles and cover designs that distinguish them. Remember, the title is an important part of your book's marketing and branding. It should be engaging, accurate, and intriguing to attract readers. Spend time brainstorming and exploring possibilities.

Do you want a subtitle? Subtitles are common and another opportunity to convince a reader to pick up your book. Keep them short. Make it clear what your book is about and what readers should expect when they read it. Don't pack the subtitle with too many keywords.

Good:
- A lesbian romantic comedy
- A vampire lesbian romance
- An age gap gold digger romance
- A Sapphic short story

- A friends to lovers romance
- A Sapphic lesbian medical romance
- A fake dating romance
  Annoying:
- Lesbian Sapphic WLW friends to lovers romantic comedy with vampires, fake dating, and gold diggers

Do you want a pen name? There are all sorts of reasons why a writer would use a pen name. Privacy and branding are the two main reasons, and here's my story.

Elizabeth Andre is a pen name. I'm not hiding or in the closet. Everyone in my life knows I'm a lesbian, and everyone knows I write and self-publish lesbian fiction. I use a pen name because I'm really an interracial lesbian couple. Elizabeth Andre is a joint enterprise between two people, and we contribute equally. There are some writing teams that put more than one name on a cover. I've always viewed this as a waste of space, and I'm not convinced readers care that much for it. I also started publishing under the name Elizabeth Andre because I was told to view a pen name as a brand and to have good boundaries around that brand, although that didn't really go as expected.

Note: There's nothing wrong with using a pen name, but you want to avoid misleading anyone or appropriation. If you are a white European American, don't use a pen name or create an author bio that makes it seem like you are from a marginalized racial or ethnic group. That's when people get into trouble. If you're a man or a straight woman writing lesbian fiction, don't pretend to be a lesbian author. It's arguably okay to be a man or a straight woman writing lesbian fiction. It's definitely not okay to pretend to be a lesbian writing lesbian fiction.

When I started self-publishing in 2014, I took seriously the idea that a pen name was a brand and that good boundaries were needed. I did not, however, take lesbian fiction seriously. I loved reading it, but I was told that lesbian fiction didn't sell. Lesbians were not supportive, and it wasn't that big of a market. *Don't waste your time on lesbian fiction,* I was told. *Focus on gay male fiction. It's a big market with lots of money to be made.*

Oh, conventional wisdom, how do I fall for this every time.

> *"Nobody knows anything."—William*
> *Goldman, Oscar-winning script writer.*

So, I worked on my gay male fiction. I'd written some of it in the 1990s, and I viewed the writing I started in 2014 as my second writing career. I devised pen names for my gay male fiction. I defined them. I kept good boundaries around what those pen names would do and would not. Then my wife wanted to write some lesbian fiction. We created a pen name, Elizabeth Andre, and I didn't take it seriously. We wrote whatever lesbian fiction we felt like—science fiction time travel romance, dark romance, young adult, sweet romantic comedy, etc. And an interesting thing happened. Our gay male fiction sold, but our lesbian fiction sold better. Much better. When we sat down and crunched the numbers, we discovered that Elizabeth Andre was responsible for 90% of our sales. We have since retired our gay male pen names, and now we have a lesbian pen name with a very messy brand, all because we were told the lesbian fiction market was too small and there wasn't any money in it. I'm always afraid of disappointing or even scaring my readers, but I'm going to move forward with what I've got.

I hate conventional wisdom and I caution you to beware of self-fulfilling prophecies. This is when you tell yourself what you expect to happen, "lesbian books don't sell," and then take action (or not) that ensures that what you've told yourself will come true, like publishing a lesbian novel and half-assing the writing, cover design, and marketing. Then the book doesn't sell, so what you've told yourself is affirmed.

Beware of internalized (and externalized) homophobia, lesbophobia, and misogyny. These are the evil concepts that underlie stupid statements like, "lesbian fiction doesn't sell."

Lesbian fiction does sell. People want to read it, and If I had to do it all over again, I wouldn't waste my time with gay male fiction. I would focus on lesbian fiction, and I would have had more than one lesbian pen name.

Ah well, best laid plans.

If it's anything that the COVID-19 pandemic taught us is that plans are so 2019. Good luck with them. I hope you pick a pen name that works for you, your fiction, and your goals.

Another comment on pen names, some genres such as mysteries and thrillers, really like authors to use only initials for their first names. Others prefer full names. Lesbian books are mostly written by people with a fully spelled out first name followed by a last name/surname.

Writing a great blurb

Your next step in your marketing plan is to write a great blurb which will capture readers' attention, entice them to explore the book further, and effectively convey the essence of the story.

I always start mine off with a hook. This could be a thought-provoking question, an intriguing statement, or a compelling scenario that immediately draws them into the story. When possible, I bold this statement.

Examples from some of my books:

- When the one person standing between you and true love is the wife you never knew you had… (*My Favorite Wife*)
- It's 1984, and there are lots of things the family of Helen Blumenstein, age 14, doesn't talk about. (*Learning to Kiss Girls*)
- It's never too late for love… (*Right Time for Love*)
- Life is better with a woman AND a dog. (*Lesbian With Dog Seeks Same*)

The next paragraph should introduce one of the protagonists. Provide a brief but vivid description of the main character, highlighting their unique qualities, struggles, or aspirations. Make readers curious about their journey and invested in their outcomes.

The paragraph after that one should introduce the other protagonist and get more into the conflict or central theme. Clearly convey the central conflict, dilemma, or theme of the story. This could be a romantic entanglement, self-discovery, overcoming adversity, or any other pivotal element that drives the narrative.

Your blurb should highlight emotional stakes. Explore the emotional journey of the characters and the potential consequences of their choices. Emphasize the emotional depth and the impact the story will have on readers' hearts and minds. Don't forget to showcase the unique aspects. Highlight any distinctive elements or unique aspects of your novel. Whether it's the setting, a fresh perspective, a unique narrative structure, or a particular theme, convey what sets your book apart from others in the genre. You also need to maintain a compelling tone. Craft the blurb's tone to match the mood of your novel. Whether it's heartwarming, intense, humorous, or thought-provoking, the tone should resonate with the target readership and accurately represent the overall atmosphere of the book.

I end my blurbs with another one-line hook. I leave readers wanting more by ending the blurb with a compelling cliffhanger, a powerful statement, or a question that creates a sense of anticipation. Make them feel the need to dive immediately into the story.

Examples from my books:

- All she has to do is find a judge basking naked in a hot tub on her day off and get to the chapel on time. (*My Favorite Wife*)
- ...even if that means being a little bit queer. (*Learning to Kiss Girls*)

- Together they navigate the rocky waters of love found when they both least expect it and discover that second chances are worth taking. (*Right Time for Love*)
- She has to find her again, even though she doesn't know her name, and begins to realize that her life will be even better with this woman in it. (*Lesbian With Dog Seeks Same*)

I know it's very tempting to fill a blurb with questions. Avoid that trap. You want a blurb filled with dramatic tension that makes readers want more. You can include a question or two but use questions sparingly. Keep it concise. Aim for a blurb that is succinct and impactful. Generally, a blurb should be around 150-250 words, providing enough information to entice readers without giving away major plot details or spoilers.

I then close the blurb with a direct statement about the book. When possible, I put that closing line in italics. More examples from my books:

- *My Favorite Wife is the first book in the lesbian romantic comedy series, Going to the Chapel. It's a sweet romance, which means all scenes stop at the bedroom door, but there are lots of laughs and maybe a few superhero sightings.*
- *Right Time for Love is the fifth book in the Lesbian Light Reads series, but each book can stand alone. This lesbian contemporary love story includes graphic sex and is intended for adults only.*
- *Lesbian With Dog Seeks Same is the third book in the Lesbian Light Reads series, but each book stands alone. This lesbian contemporary love story includes graphic sex and is intended for adults only.*

Note: Many authors hate writing blurbs, and I don't blame them. Some are paying expert blurb writers for the task. Others have started using AI to write their blurbs.

Book categories and keywords

Your next step is to categorize your book. According to K-Lytics, there are over fifty LGBTQ categories. However, there are very few specific lesbian categories. Most lesbian books fall into either "lesbian fiction," "lesbian romance," or both. Lesbian erotica is also a possibility, although there are some distinctions by platform that I will get into in Chapters Twelve through Twenty.

Now it's time to select keywords. Not all platforms allow keywords, but for those that do it's important to come up with a good list. There are a lot of keyword generating tools. I haven't used them, but others may find them useful. Generally, keywords should directly relate to your book's plot, themes, characters, or setting. Think about emotions, conflicts, relationships, and any unique elements of your story. Consider both specific and broader terms. Don't forget to include tropes.

Before I brainstorm my keywords, my trick is to start with Amazon. I type my possible keywords into the Amazon search bar and let Amazon's autocomplete generate suggestions. These are some of my favorite keywords, and you can use them too if they relate to your book:

- happy ending
- beautiful women
- lesbian
- pride
- books
- love
- lgbt
- lgbtq+
- wlw
- hea
- lesfic
- fiction

- novel
- Ownvoices

Only use the term, "ownvoices," if it's true. Ownvoices means your book includes characters from under-represented/marginalized groups and you share their identity.

Note: The goal is not to get your book in front of the greatest number of people. The goal is to get your book in front of the people who are most likely to want to buy your book.

Creating a series and all about pre-orders

Should you create a series? Maybe. There's nothing wrong with stand-alone books. Series can be a bit easier to market because readers hopefully start with book one and read all the books in the series. Then again, a long series may be a block for a reader. They may not be interested in book nine if they don't like book one. If book six falls flat, readers may never get to book seven. If readers see a book marked as "volume 1" and there isn't yet a "volume 2," they may avoid it in fear that the series has been abandoned by its author. I have several series connected either by a theme or common characters, and they work well for me. Several authors do quite well financially by rapidly releasing several books in a series in a short amount of time.

Note: Generally speaking, readers hate cliffhangers, especially if the next book takes months or years to be published or is never published at all. I avoid cliffhangers.

Should you have a pre-order period? Maybe. It has its pluses and minuses. I've had mixed experiences with them. The pluses:

- You have a link to share as part of your promotional efforts.
- On Amazon, it can negatively impact your rank if you don't have consistent sales during your pre-order

period. A high sales rank can improve your sales on that platform.

- You know exactly when your book will be published. The time between uploading your book to a vendor and it being published ranges from 24-72 hours and can be longer. It can also be shorter. When I first started self-publishing, I liked a two-week pre-order period. The one time I did three months, it was a disaster. I currently do four days or no pre-order period. The choice is yours. To get around not having an official pre-order but still wanting a link to share, some writers publish their paperback first, use that link for marketing, and then publish the e-book with a pre-order period, using the e-book publishing date as the book's official publishing date. Have fun with it. Experiment until you find something that works for you.

Setting your price

Setting a price for your book is yet another subject of endless debate among self-published authors. There are differences in royalty rates for different prices, and those vary by vendor. I will get into those variances in Chapters Twelve through Twenty. I like a price that's high enough that readers may find a sale particularly appealing. Some authors price their first e-book in a series at 99 cents or free. The e-books in the top ten of the lesbian fiction bestseller list range in price from 99 cents to $9.99. Also, keep in mind that some readers will access your e-book through a subscription service like Kindle Unlimited or Scribd. They may also access it through their library, so the price may not matter that much to them.

Here's how I price my e-books:
- I have a small number of short stories (6,000-8,000 words) priced at 99 cents.

- I sometimes price the first book in my series at 99 cents but not always.
- My novellas (15,000-25,000 words) are usually $2.99-$4.99.
- My novels (anything over 40,000 words) range in price from $4.99-$9.99, with the price determined by book length and genre.
- When releasing a new book, I've had good experiences with setting the price at 99 cents for the first week and then increasing the price.
- When participating in a sale, I mark my books down to 99 cents or $2.99.
- I would generally avoid the $1.99 price, which is a terrible one. It's ugly, and the royalty rates are terrible.
- Prices for libraries should be two to three times the retail price.
  Here is how I price my paper books:
- I price paperbacks from $10.95-$21.95, depending on length. When selling books in person (discussed in Chapter Ten), I discount these books to either $10 or $15 and offer discounts if someone buys more than one.
- I price my hardcovers at $20.95. I've never actually sold a hardcover book. I'm not even sure how many people still read hardcovers, but I have them available if someone wants one.
  Here's how I price my audiobooks:
  I've just started making audiobooks. Generally speaking, these are the recommended prices for human-narrated audiobooks. AI-narrated audiobooks should be half that or less.
- Under 1 hour: under $7
- 1–3 hours: $7–$10
- 3–5 hours: $10–$20
- 5–10 hours: $15–$25
- 10–20 hours: $20–$30

- Over 20 hours: $25–$35

What next?

You could try some push marketing, which I cover in Chapter Nine, but you don't have to. I will say pull marketing has become less effective over the years as the market has become more crowded, but all is not lost. Pull marketing still has a lot of power, and it can be both subtle and effective. Besides, saying "buy my book" all the time is obnoxious and not that effective in the modern world. You should do nearly everything involved in pull marketing, but everything in push marketing is optional.

You could produce another book, which can be a very powerful marketing tool. Always update the back matter for your books with buy links for your other books. You want readers to go from one book to the next. I like to create universal Amazon links with Booklinker. Books2Read, owned by Draft2Digital, is also popular. Both of these are free to use. For Books2Read you don't also have to be published on Draft2Digital.

CHAPTER NINE

Mastering push marketing

This is the part of your marketing plan that people are thinking of when they ask about what you do to sell books. It probably leads to about 20% of my sales long term. Push marketing can involve sending out advance review copies (ARCs) to solicit early reviews, alerting relevant websites to your book's existence, submitting your book to various awards, alerting your newsletter subscribers, posting on your favorite social media channels, and advertising your book on several platforms.

Push marketing is not as awful as it sounds. Don't be scared. This is your opportunity to tell readers, who you know will really love your book if they just gave it a chance, all about your fabulous book.

Note (yes, this is repeated from the last chapter because it's important): There are a million things you can do to market your book. You don't have to do everything. You should probably keep your marketing list short. It's better to do one marketing strategy well than to do ten poorly. Don't let anyone tell you that you **MUST** do one thing or another, especially if they've never even written a book let alone published one. Do what makes you comfortable. If you are comfortable on Facebook and your readers are there, stay there. If you enjoy making TikTok videos, continue having fun there. If you hate both of those platforms, don't feel like you have to join them.

And another note (specific to push marketing): Try to avoid creating a marketing spiral that only gets bigger and leads to nowhere. What you want is a funnel that leads to your book.

What I mean by that: You publish a book and start marketing it. Then you write a blog post and make a book trailer. Do the blog post and book trailer lead people to your book (funnel) or are you now promoting a book, a trailer, and a blog post (spiral)? It's important to think about your digital infrastructure. This is addressed later in this chapter.

One more note: Selling to friends and family is not a business strategy, and you might end up annoying them.

Tip: Because there are so many things you can do to market your book, I make a priority list of possibilities. On the top of the list are the things with the most payoff. Then I set a timer. I go through the list as best I can. When the timer goes off, my marketing efforts are done for the day, no matter how far I've actually gotten through my list. I'm done. I've done enough.

Do not let marketing suck up all of your time and energy, and never forget your goals. Is your ultimate goal book sales or more followers on a particular social media platform? Whatever marketing you do should be in alignment with your goals—not anyone else's. Your goals can change, but they should always be yours and yours alone.

Do not let this marketing phase distract you. I know that's easier said than done, but when in doubt reread the preceding paragraph.

Important core concept: It is better to have ten diehard fans than a thousand indifferent social media followers. Be focused. You can buy an hour on a digital billboard in Times Square in New York for a few hundred dollars, but only do that if your dream is to have your book on a digital billboard in Times Square for an hour. The people who see your ad are unlikely to be your target audience, and it probably won't result in many, if any, sales. A small event full of your target audience is far more valuable than a large event with only a few people who might be marginally interested.

Getting reviews

Authors can get quite obsessed with reviews, and I understand why. You've put all this work and care into your book. No one likes to hear bad things said about their child, I mean their book, and hearing good things can make your week. Do your best to step away and not take anything personally.

Basic rules when it comes to reviews
Reviews are for readers. They are not for authors. They are not for you.

If someone gives you a bad review, do not engage them. Do not respond. Do not bad mouth them. Do not take revenge. LEAVE THEM ALONE.

If someone gives you a good review, don't engage them either. That review is still not for you. If you do contact them, tread carefully and don't be surprised if they don't respond. I will talk about possible exceptions in my section on superfans.

Just because a review is one or two stars doesn't mean there's no valuable information for someone who might be interested in your book. For example, I wear minimalist shoes. These are shoes that are completely flat with no heel and no support. I know that when someone gives a one- or two- star review to a pair of shoes and complains that they have no support, that's the shoe for me. A reviewer complaining about too much sex in one of my books may pique the interest of someone who thinks there should be even more sex.

Reviews may not make any sense to you, and they don't have to. I once had a reviewer complain that I got time travel wrong in my book, *The Time Slip Girl* (spoiler alert: you can't actually travel through time, and therefore, there is no way to do it wrong in fiction).

If reviews bother you too much, don't read them. They're not for you anyway.

So, how do you get reviews?

I run the Lesfic ARC Club on Facebook. This is a Facebook group where authors can post requests for reviews and readers can request a free copy. Reviews are then posted on various publishing platforms, Goodreads, other reader sites, and/or the reviewer's own website. I approve the posts that appear in the group and keep it focused. I don't allow general discussions of reviews or lesbian fiction, but I don't enforce the "advance" part of ARC that heavily. If your book is coming soon or already out, you are welcome to post a request for reviews. I also don't enforce a particularly rigid definition of lesbian fiction. As long as your book doesn't have a picture of a shirtless man on the cover, I'll probably approve your post.

Note: Even if you give someone an ARC, you cannot require them to review it. If they do not review it at all, don't hassle them. Leave them alone.

I've seen authors post requests for reviews in other Facebook groups and on other social media platforms. It's also common for an author to post a review request in the back of their books.

IMPORTANT: Do not review your own book and pretend that the review is from someone else. That's gross.

Alerting websites and bloggers

Once again, stay focused. There are several lesbian fiction websites that I will mention below, and they are your best bet for getting reviews and other publicity for your books.

Note: Burnout among reviewers and others who write about the lesbian literary world is high. Be nice to them.

You can send your book out to websites and bloggers that, while they don't have a specific interest in lesbian fiction, may have an interest in your genre. For example, those who write generally about mystery fiction or romance fiction may review your lesbian romance or lesbian mystery or mention it on their website.

Always remember your reader. Are your potential readers reading those websites for tips on what they should read next? I would never try to dissuade anyone from attempting to get mainstream success and attention. I'm just saying your time is limited. It's important to be stingy with your time.

There are some people who will never give your book a chance because it has lesbians or other queers in it. Let them go. Focus on people who want you.

Anyway, here are some websites that review lesbian fiction that were active when I wrote this book:

The Lesbrary has reviews and articles about lesbian fiction, and it is one of the top lesbian fiction blogs. They welcome submissions of books for review, and I've had a couple of my books reviewed by them. You can submit your book and take the chance that one of their contributors will pick it to review, or you can pay $100 and guarantee that someone will review it and post it on the blog, Amazon, and Goodreads. In either case, the review will be an honest one. Other options include paying $50 for a video that incorporates your book. Although not a review, the video will be posted on the Lesbrary website and TikTok. Ads on the website are reasonably priced.

Note: Should you pay for a review? This is a matter of debate in the self-publishing community, and the answer is maybe. I never have, but some authors say it's worth it. Its value, however, can vary. Paying for a guaranteed review in the Lesbrary is probably worth it, especially if it's a good one (no guarantee of that). I'm more dubious about other paid review services.

The Lesbian Review is a website that does exactly what it says. They have a team of contributors that review lesbian fiction. They've reviewed several of my books, and they have a form on their website for review consideration. Advertising is also available at reasonable rates, but there's no link between ads and reviews. You can't buy a review. You can buy an ad.

LezReviewBooks is another review website. They haven't reviewed my books, but they also receive a lot of review copies. Submit your book and cross your fingers. This website also has a list of resources for lesbian authors.

Rainbow Round Table Book and Media Reviews is a website run by the American Library Association. I have submitted my books many times, and many of my books are in libraries. Alas, I've never convinced the Rainbow Round Table to review any of my books. The submission form is easy to use. I do recommend submitting your books to them. I hope you have better luck than I have had.

Lambda Literary Review is a publication I think of fondly. I wrote for them in the 1990s back when they were on paper. I haven't convinced them to review any of my books yet, but I remain hopeful.

There are others, but these are some of the biggest. Other important websites for lesfic authors include:

I Heart SapphFic doesn't review lesbian fiction, but this website does have loads of opportunities for promoting your book. Your first step is to add your book to their bookfinder database of Sapphic fiction. They send out regular newsletters with new releases, and you should make sure they announce yours. They also have periodic sales featuring dozens of discounted lesbian books and reading challenges. These are worth participating in. You can pay for ads on the site, and they are reasonably priced.

IReadIndies International, Inc., is a non-profit serving indie authors of Sapphic literature. This organization works to bring more visibility, recognition, and support to self-published authors. They do a lot of good collaborative work, and they are worth checking out. They have some interesting no-cost promotional opportunities.

The Sapphic Quill is run by lesbian fiction author Jae. The website provides advice for lesfic authors as well as many no-cost promotional opportunities.

There are also several paid promotion sites that you should consider.

MyQueerSapphFic offers paid promotional opportunities and is probably the best opportunity for queer, lesbian, and Sapphic books. Their promotions for discounted books and new releases are reasonably priced.

BookBub is a behemoth in the book promotions world, and if you haven't heard of them, you should check them out. They have numerous paid opportunities and a few free ones. The paid opportunities are highly competitive and expensive but generally worth it if you are lucky enough to land one. The one you want is "featured deal." For this opportunity you deeply discount your book, and you pay BookBub to promote it. Most people make the cost of the promotion back and then some through sales of the discounted book and additional sales of books by the same pen name at full price. We've landed about a half dozen BookBub featured deals over the years, and they've usually done well for us. **Note:** BookBub has an LGBTQ+ category but not a specific lesbian category.

There are numerous other paid newsletter and promotion services. I haven't had good luck with the ones that don't have dedicated lesbian or LGBTQ+ categories, but your mileage may vary.

Note: Websites change all the time. Websites that reviewed and promoted my books a decade ago are long gone, and new ones have emerged.

Submitting to awards

"I can't deny the fact that you like me. Right now, you like me!"—Sally Field after winning an Oscar for the movie Places in the Heart

When I was a kid, I dreamed of writing a bestselling book that would be made into an Oscar-winning movie. My speech would thank my parents, my hometown of Chicago, and my high school math teacher for always believing in me. I've had bestselling books, but alas, no movie deals, yet, and hence no Oscar. I do have a Goldie from the Golden Crown Literary Society, the organization for lesbian writers and the readers who love them, and some other awards. Awards can be valuable, especially if you win, but much like everything else in self-publishing, be careful how much money and time you devote to them.

Core concepts for awards: I'm going to list several award programs. Keep your goals in mind when considering entering. If your goal is greater sales, only enter the most notable award programs that have the most reader recognition. If what you want is an award, submit your book for the awards it is most likely to win. Most awards cost money. Consider the potential impact if you win but also if you don't.

Note: I have seen some books promoted with the tagline that the book is a nominee for this award or that. That means the author or publisher nominated the book for the award. You can mention this as part of your marketing, but I don't. It feels tacky.

Scam alert: Some award programs charge large amounts of money for awards of no or minimal value. Some award programs are a way for fee-charging literary agencies to attract authors. They charge high fees for the award. The prize is representation, which also comes with high fees. This is also a ploy used by organizations selling editing services. You win the award, but for a fee, they claim they will make your work even better. There are contest mills. These are companies that make money via entry fees. Some promise large prizes, but if you read the fine print, you'll note that the contest reserves the right to award prizes on a pro-rated basis. This means that the prize amounts are determined by the number of entrants. This guarantees that the company makes a profit no matter what. To learn more about predatory award programs, take a look at Writer Beware®, which is run by the Science Fiction & Fantasy Writers Association.

The following are reputable award programs that may be receptive to your lesbian novel.

Goldie Awards are run by the Golden Crown Literary Society (GCLS), and I've won one. The GCLS awards recognize excellence in women-loving-women and Sapphic literature. There are awards for writing and cover design. There is an entrance fee, but it's reasonable.

Stonewall Book Awards were first awarded in 1971. This awards program is run by the American Library Association's Rainbow Round Table. No entry fee and anyone can nominate a book for consideration via an online form. I have nominated my books but have not won.

Lambda Literary Awards, also known as the "Lammys," celebrate LGBTQ+ literature across various categories, including fiction, non-fiction, poetry, and more. There is a fee. The awards dinner in New York has always looked fun. Becoming a finalist is an honor. Winning a Lambda is a big deal. I dream of winning one.

There are other award programs, but these are the ones I recommend and regularly enter.

Building your digital infrastructure

You've written the book. You've published the book. You've written great metadata and a great blurb. You're getting reviews. You've submitted to a couple of award programs, and fingers crossed, maybe you'll win something. I'm about to get more into the weeds about what people traditionally associate with marketing (websites, email newsletters, social media, and advertising), but before I do that, I'd like to take a brief step back to talk about your digital infrastructure.

Most people, when they think about an author's online presence, think of a website. I'd like to get you away from that thinking to think more holistically about your digital infrastructure. Here's why: I mentioned earlier the concept of a marketing spiral versus a marketing funnel. What you want to avoid is publishing a book, building a website, creating book trailers, building substantial followings on one or more social media platforms, and having them all lead to each other. That puts you in a position of having to market a book, a website, a book trailer, and one or more social media identities. Welcome to a market spiral. It will only get bigger as you add more stuff. The reader won't know where to go and will never end up where you want them to be. There won't be any organic growth. I guarantee you will end up frustrated.

Do not lose heart. It is possible to create a digital infrastructure that funnels readers to your goal.

For example, my priority is book sales. As much as possible, I lead readers to an opportunity to buy one of my books. If I don't lead them there, I lead them to a sign-on page for my email newsletter. The email newsletter is important because it's a communication vehicle that I control. I own the email addresses. It is possible for readers to follow me on various publishing platforms. This is not a bad thing. The platform usually alerts followers to the existence of a new release, but not always. You can't control the communication. You can't add to it if you have something else to say, and you can't download a list of followers and communicate with them as you see fit. You should utilize built in vendor marketing tools, but when in doubt, lead readers to your email newsletter.

But what about a website? You could have a website, but if you don't have one, I wouldn't fret too much. You should have some way to be discoverable and for readers to contact you. It's okay if that's a Facebook page and Facebook Messenger, especially when you're just starting out.

Note: Once you have built your digital infrastructure, you will need to reevaluate it periodically. The way people discover the books they want to read and connect with authors changes all the time.

Website

I'm not saying you can't have a website. You may want one at some point, but don't let it stress you out. And don't let anyone tell you that you **MUST** have a website.

NEVER CREATE THE WEBSITE BEFORE YOU'VE WRITTEN THE BOOK.

But, if you insist, here's what you need to know.

You can hire someone to create a website, but, especially when you are just starting out, you will most likely make your own.

Key points:

- **Domain:** Choose a domain name (e.g., yourauthorname.com) that is easy to remember and reflects your brand. Register the domain through a reliable domain registrar. I've used name.com, but there are numerous companies that provide this service.
- **Website Platform:** Select a website platform or content management system (CMS) that suits your needs and technical comfort level. Popular options

include WordPress, Wix, Squarespace, Weebly, and Carrd. These platforms offer user-friendly interfaces and customizable templates.

- **Design and Branding:** Create a visually appealing website that reflects your brand and the genre you write in. Choose a clean layout, readable fonts, and complementary colors.

So, what should you put on your website, especially if you only have one book? You can probably get away with a one-page "landing page" with your pen name and brief bio, information about your book, links to buy your book, and a link to subscribe to your newsletter.

Never miss a chance to collect someone's contact details.

You can also include links to your social media handles, the fewer the better. Seriously, you don't need to be on all platforms, and I'll discuss that in more depth later in this chapter.

Ensure your website is optimized for mobile devices. More and more people do nearly everything on their phones and spend very little time on a laptop and certainly not a desktop.

Implement basic search engine optimization (SEO) techniques to improve the visibility of your website in search engine results.

Regularly update your website with fresh content, new book releases, and author news. Keep your site secure and perform routine backups to protect your content.

Remember, while creating a website can be exciting, focus on providing a user-friendly experience and showcasing your work effectively. If you're not comfortable with web design or maintenance, consider hiring a professional web designer or developer to help you create a polished and functional website.

Alert: If you hire someone to create your website, make sure you have access to everything and everything is in your name. Get all the assets that you need. Don't get stuck with a dead website because the person who built it has disappeared.

Email newsletters

Debate periodically flares as to the usefulness of an email newsletter. Should you get a Discord server? Focus on Instagram? It depends. Are you comfortable on Discord? If not, either get more comfortable or get an email newsletter. What about Instagram, which is very popular? You don't own your contacts on Instagram, and if that platform changes its algorithm, your fans may not see what you want them to see.

I'm still a fan of email newsletters. I use MailerLite_for mine, which is a pretty user-friendly platform. Other popular options include SendFox and Mailchimp.

Remember that you have to have a list of 15 people before you can build to a list of a hundred. You have to have a list of a hundred before you can build to a thousand. It's okay if your list is small. It will grow if you let it.

Also, 15 dedicated fans are far more valuable (and fun) than a thousand indifferent subscribers.

So, how do you grow your email list?

When I sell books in person (more details in Chapter Ten), I have an email sign-up sheet and a pen, and I see a growing number of authors posting or handing out QR codes. I put a sign-up link in the front and back of my books. For my e-books, it's a live link. For my paperbacks, I use a QR code that takes readers to the newsletter sign-up pages. You can create a free QR code in Google Chrome or Canva. When I first started self-publishing, I just promised readers that I would keep in touch and that subscribing meant they wouldn't miss anything. I now offer an exclusive short story such as a prequel or bonus material. This is often referred to as a reader magnet.

One service to consider is BookFunnel. This platform hosts numerous group promotions organized by authors, including authors of Sapphic fiction. You create a sign-up page on the website offering something in exchange for a reader's email—usually a reader magnet. All the participating authors send out links to the group promotion, including you. The parameters of the promotion are set by the organizer. I've gained hundreds of newsletter subscribers this way. BookFunnel can also be used to securely deliver advance review copies, and their prices are reasonable.

A note about newsletter swaps: This is when one author promotes another author in their newsletter. It's usually in exchange for the other author doing the same. I would use this strategy cautiously. Your newsletter readers have signed up to hear about you. Be judicious about what you include in your newsletter. You don't want to turn them off and lead them to unsubscribing by including irrelevant or low-quality content.

Social media

Social media is either an incredible time suck or a gift to authors who can promote their books directly to readers. Your truth is probably somewhere between the two.

Note: If you don't want to be on certain platforms or don't want to be on social media at all, then don't. Don't let anyone tell you that you have to do one thing or another. It is better to do one thing well than to do ten things poorly. If you do participate, set limits on time, number of platforms, and other variables.

Also note: There are loads of "experts" advising to consistently post at least daily on your chosen platform, use trending memes, use trending sounds, or whatever the hot social media advice is of the moment. None of this is necessarily bad advice, but it's also not necessarily good advice. Always remember:

> *"Nobody knows anything."—William*
> *Goldman, Oscar-winning script writer.*

Key concepts:
- If you are going to spend time on social media, identify where your readers hang out and hang out there.
- If the social media platform is for readers, don't be a creepy author and harass your readers. Let them read in peace.
- Have something else to say besides "buy my book."
- It's okay to use a pseudonym. It's not okay to pretend to be someone else, especially if you are pretending to be from a community historically excluded from publishing. If you're a white lesbian from a wealthy part of the U.S., don't pretend to be a Black lesbian from anywhere, wealthy or poor. Just don't. Yes, it's arguably okay to be a cisgender man writing lesbian fiction. It's never okay for a cisgender man to pretend to be a lesbian.
- Social media changes all the time. Be nimble.
- Play nice. Don't be a jerk.

Expert advice conflicts as far as what you should post when you are trying to market a book. Some advocate focusing on your book, and nothing else. Others advocate a more personable approach and advise posting about your book and your pets or your crafts. I post a mix depending on my mood and what I have going on. I sew and sometimes I post my crafts. I bake and sometimes I post my pastries. Sometimes I talk about writing. Other times I talk more generally about LGBTQ+ issues. Sometimes I talk about my books. I try to stay "on brand," which for me means staying focused on what is important to lesbian readers and the people who love them. For example, I have medical expertise. Unless I've finally finished that medical thriller I've always wanted to write, you're probably not going to hear much about health care in my social media posts, although I did post recently about scurvy and linked it to lesbian literature and a couple of my book covers, so there's that.

Some tips by specific platform:

X (formerly Twitter): I've been on Twitter for about a decade, although ownership changes in 2022 mean that quite a few people have left the platform. I've had modest success posting links to my books using the hashtags #SapphicFiction, #Lesfic, #QueerReads, and others as appropriate. Don't use too many hashtags, three max. I make sure my banner and profile photo advertise my most recent books. I include a link to subscribe to my email newsletter in my profile. I try to spend about five minutes a few times a week interacting with other accounts on the platform. I post text, links, a photo, and/or a video when I have something to say. Don't forget to include alt-text if you post a photo for those who are visually impaired. My most popular tweet was a link to a compilation I created in 2020 of "Black lesbian (and bi, queer, trans, and non-binary) fiction authors you should know." That was fun to make, although my experience highlights how hard it is to get people to do more than "like" a social media post. That tweet got 36,808 impressions and 1,428 engagements. Alas, only 358 people actually clicked on the link to read the list.

Facebook: I have a personal account under my real name and a page for my pen name. Facebook isn't super crazy about people posting commercial links on their personal page, but I don't do it too often, so I've been okay. I'm mostly bragging anyway because selling to friends and family is not a business strategy and can get pretty annoying. On my pen name's page, the banner and profile photo advertise my most recent books. I also include my contact email and a link to sign up for my email newsletter. I post text, links, photos, and/or videos when I have something to say. Lately, I've been posting more Facebook Reels

(Facebook's answer to TikTok), and those have been getting good traction. One video got more than 4,000 views, although most of them get a hundred to 500 views. Some Facebook groups will allow pages to be members, but not all. I recommend against posting the same thing in dozens of groups, especially if those groups don't seem that active. That's a waste of time. Stick to the groups with more interaction and always follow the group's rules when posting anything. I use the hashtags #lesfic, #sapphic, #lesbian, and others as appropriate. My most popular post was a 16-second reel where I told a story about meeting a young lesbian who was impressed by the 45 rpm record adapter I wore on a necklace around my neck and the fact that I was with my wife of 15 years.

TikTok: This platform didn't exist when I started self-publishing, and now Booktok is huge. Huge, I tell you! TikTok is also lesbian heaven. There are so many lesbians on this app, and there are so many readers. I enjoy it immensely. Learning how to make short videos is easier than it sounds, and once you start you will get better quickly with every video you make. If you're going to use the account to promote your book, make sure you set it up as a business account. This does limit the music and other TikTok-approved sounds you can use, but that's not that big of a deal. You can post one or more photos or short videos. I sometimes shoot the videos in the app itself, adding music, stickers, text, and closed captions. Sometimes I create the videos in Canva or CapCut. The latter is owned by TikTok, and some believe the app favors videos either shot in TikTok or CapCut. I have a relevant username (elizabethandrelesfic). I post my pronouns. Once you have over a thousand followers you can post a live link to your profile. My videos get between a hundred and 800 views, although I just had one break 8,000. There's some debate as to the perfect number of hashtags. Some fill the description with as many hashtags as possible. Others limit themselves to ten. I recommend always having some kind of text description of the video in addition to hashtags and having some text as a part of the video. Captions are recommended. Some people watch TikTok without sound. Others are deaf. Always keep accessibility in mind. The "TikTok for Authors" group on Facebook has some good tips. My favorite hashtags are #lesfic, #sapphicreads, #lesbianbooktok, #fyp, #lesbianbooks, #sapphicauthor, #sapphicbooks, and #lesbiansoftiktok. One of my most viewed videos is one where I talk about my book cover, which features a grapefruit being fingered suggestively, and the need for lesbians to keep eating citrus in order to prevent scurvy.

Random trivia from my life as a medical writer: A half dozen people in the U.S die of scurvy every year. Eating your citrus is no joke.

But the video was pretty funny.

A note on repurposing TikTok content: Some platforms really hate the TikTok watermark, and I think it's tacky to have videos with the TikTok watermark on other platforms. If you can get a version of your video without the TikTok watermark, that would be good to repurpose for other platforms.

Instagram: I know Instagram is super popular, but I've never liked it that much. Nonetheless, I'm on it. I post images and videos. I use the hashtags #bookstagram and #lesfic. If you like Instagram, maybe you could give me a few tips some day?

These are the social media platforms I've been using. You can be on others such as Pinterest, Tumblr, YouTube, or Mastodon, but be stingy with your time. Don't let social media activity detract from your writing.

Note: You can do everything right on social media and get no likes, follows, or kind words. You can do everything wrong and get all the attention you ever dreamed of (and some you didn't). Life is random. Social media is even more random, and it's impossible to control what's going to blow up and what isn't. Here are a couple of case studies to illustrate that point.

Case study: Doing it right
On December 4, 2022, fantasy author Chelsea Banning posted on Twitter:

> *"Only 2 people came to my author signing yesterday, so I was pretty bummed about it. Especially as 37 people responded 'going' to the event. Kind of upset, honestly, and a little embarrassed."*

This became a Tweet heard around the world. Bestselling authors such as Neil Gaiman, Margaret Atwood, Stephen King, and Jodi Picoult commented and retweeted with their own book-signing horror stories. The tweet went viral with 3,887 comments, 7,718 retweets, and 78,900 likes. Her book Of *Crowns and Legends* became a bestseller. Major media outlets wrote about her newfound success. Her subsequent book signings—that she invited other authors to—were packed.

Moral of the story: Chelsea Banning was honest and authentic, and it paid off. She also shared her newfound fame with other authors, which makes me like her even more.

Note: Stuff like this cannot be planned, and what happened was unexpected.

Also note: I do not know Chelsea Banning, but I've enjoyed seeing her on social media.

Case studies: Doing it wrong
At the end of May 2023, Sarah Stusek, a first-time author who wrote the young adult novel *Three Rivers*, made a TikTok video where she called a reviewer who gave her a four-star review a "bitch." She complained that the four-star review had ruined her streak of five-star reviews. When the

negative reactions multiplied, she followed up that video with another one where she said that she was a comedian and people just couldn't take a joke. The reader community retaliated. As of the middle of June 2023, this book still had 15 five-star reviews and one four-star review on Goodreads but had also garnered 553 one-star reviews for an overall rating of 1.11.

DO NOT RESPOND TO REVIEWERS. IF YOU SAY SOMETHING STUPID, APOLOGIZE PROPERLY.

Nurturing superfans

I love superfans. These are people who are not related to you but will still read whatever you write. They give you good reviews. They tell other people to buy and read your books.

So, how do you find them? I found mine by talking to people on a regular basis, usually online, and developing a relationship with them. My superfans get early personalized notes when I am releasing a new book. I give them freebies. I treat them with the love and respect they deserve. They don't always respond to me. That's okay. Life happens, but they have done me right. I try to do right by them. Some authors refer to their superfans as members of their "street teams" and create designated newsletters or online communities just for them.

Advertising

Should you pay to advertise your book?

Maybe. Some people do very well and make a profit by paying for advertising. Other people sell a lot of books, but never pay for advertising. Like anything, your mileage may vary. Be cautious with your money and your time. I covered paid newsletters earlier in this chapter, but it's also very common for self-published authors to pay for cost-per-click (CPC) advertising on Facebook, TikTok, BookBub, and Amazon. There are lots of other CPC platforms, but those seem to be the ones that get the most bang for the buck for authors.

The details of advertising on Amazon are included in Chapter Thirteen about publishing on Kindle Direct Publishing. I have advertised on Amazon, but not on other platforms. To learn more about advertising on Facebook or other social media platforms, I recommend checking out various posts in the 20booksto50k® group on Facebook, an excellent resource for all things self-publishing. Written Word Media has an ad management service for Facebook and Amazon on its list of offerings for self-published authors.

Hopefully your book is now a bestseller, but if it's not, that's okay. I'm so proud of you. You wrote a book. You published a book. You marketed a book. You now know that this process is both easy and hard. I hope you have as much fun with it as I do.

Keep in mind that marketing changes constantly. It's important to experiment with different marketing strategies and find the ones that work best for you and your book. There are a million things you can do, and I hope I haven't overwhelmed you. Pick one thing to start. Don't agonize over it. Do what you can. The truth is you won't know what triggers most sales. I read a blog post years ago by a musician who said the internet was like a magic cow. If you feed it good stuff, it poops gold, but it's better to not know what happens in between. You may or may not make gold from your books but focus on writing. That's what's important. Do the marketing that you can. I have a little more to say about marketing in Chapters Ten and Eleven, and then I'll get into the details of the marketing opportunities offered by various publishing platforms in Chapters Twelve through Twenty.

CHAPTER TEN

In-person events

In-person events definitely fall under the push marketing category but deserve their own chapter. As with everything else in self-publishing, keep your goals in mind and don't let anyone tell you that you have to do in-person events. They're not for everyone, and for some, they represent their worst nightmare. For others, they're what they've always dreamed of. In-person events include readings which usually happen at a bookstore, although I've occasionally done them at parties upon request. They also include appearing on panels at conferences and other events. Additionally, you can sell your books at fairs and festivals.

Readings and panels

Whether you read your books at various events or participate in relevant panel discussions at conventions should depend on your goals. My priority is book sales, so I tend to keep my public appearances to a minimum because they can take up a lot of time and tend not to be that good for sales. Besides, if you appear everywhere all of the time, people take you for granted. Public appearances can be an awful lot of fun, though.

My very first in-person appearance as an author was at Gaylaxicon, an LGBTQ+ science fiction, fantasy, and horror convention in Minneapolis in 2016. I decided not to exhibit in the vendor mart because I wasn't ready. I didn't feel I had enough books (**Note:** There's nothing wrong with having one book to sell), but we did volunteer to be on panels if need be. I printed up flyers with discount codes for our books that could be used on Smashwords, a publishing aggregator that I discuss in Chapter Eighteen. I left these flyers on a table in the registration area, and the organizer asked me and my wife to present on self-publishing; sex, love, and romance in science fiction; and lesbians in science fiction.

We were told these topics less than a week before the event.

Note: Events like Gaylaxicon are often planned by a small group of dedicated volunteers and sometimes even just one person doing their best. Don't hassle them. Don't say nasty things about them. Without people like these dedicated volunteers, the world would be a much worse place. I appreciate their hard work.

Onward. The self-publishing panel was a blast. We had a handout and answered lots of questions. The sex, love, and romance panel was, thankfully, not recorded, but it was wild. What happens at Gaylaxicon stays at Gaylaxicon. We had no idea what to do for the lesbians and science fiction panel, but we recruited another conference attendee to join us. Then we peppered the audience with questions about what they wanted to see in lesbian science fiction and mostly let them talk among themselves.

The flyers had an interesting impact on sales. Nobody used the discount codes on Smashwords, and these flyers did not impact sales on that platform. However, the sales of these books at full price increased on Amazon.

Lesson: E-book readers are more likely to purchase from their preferred platform than use a coupon that saves them a dollar or two on a different platform.

Fairs and festivals

There are some self-published authors who sell almost all of their books in person, and that works for them. There are some who never sell in-person. I have some in-person sales, and I choose my festivals and fairs carefully. To be honest, I don't have the energy to spend three 12-hour days selling books, especially if it's a hot day. I choose my in-person selling opportunities based on total cost (travel, food, drink, books, table, incidentals), number of potential customers, and the amount of time required. I prefer my in-person selling events to be no more than six hours on one day. If you want to sell books over a longer time period, good for you. I recommend having at least one friend or family member to help you out, or at the bare minimum give you an opportunity for a bathroom break.

As of yet, I have only sold paperbacks in person, and I have done well. KDP prints my paperbacks, although many self-published authors get their paperbacks from Bookvault (which has some interesting printing options from spiral bound to hardbacks with foil blocking), IngramSpark, the Book Patch, 48 hour books, and Lulu. Some even work with local printers.

I make pricing as simple as possible and offer a discount for buying sets of books. For example, most of my paperbacks cost $10.95-$21.95 per copy when bought from an online vendor. In person, I charge $10, $15, or $20 each with discounts for buying more than one. I include the tax within the price. I take credit cards and do so through Square. Yes, you have to pay a modest processing fee, but that is far less expensive than a lost sale. Other sellers take

Venmo, Zelle, some other electronic money processing service, or cash. I also take cash and keeping the pricing simple means I only need a wad of five-dollar bills to provide good change. The split between people paying cash and those paying with a credit card is 50/50 at most events, although some events are primarily credit card with very little cash changing hands. Be prepared. Not taking credit cards or not having change can mean a lost sale.

Upon request, I sign the books that people have bought.

I can get hardcovers of several of my books, but I haven't tested out how well they would sell in person. I also haven't heard from other authors who have had success selling hardcovers in person. This doesn't mean you can't, or you won't be successful selling hardcovers in person. It does mean that if you attempt to do this, I would love to hear your experiences.

It is possible to sell digital items. I've seen authors load e-books and audiobooks onto a flash drive, which is usually customized in some way, and sell the flash drive. I also know that some authors upload e-books and audiobooks to Bookfunnel or some other digital delivery service. They then print out cards with information about the book, a code that can be redeemed for a copy, and information about how to download. I have not done this yet, but I intend to do so in the future.

I also recommend having promotional cards for your books. For example, if someone seems interested in one book but they don't buy it, give them the promotional card so they can buy the book later. If they do buy one or more books, I give them promotional cards for my other books. I ended up getting a stack of refrigerator magnets at a deep discount for one of my books. I hand them out as well. I don't know how effective turning my readers' refrigerators into billboards for my books has been, but it's been fun. Also, the magnets were cheap.

The most important thing you need to have is an email sign-up sheet. You can print out a piece of paper with columns headlined, "name," "email," and "I give permission for (your name) to email me," attach it to a clipboard, and keep pens nearby. Or you can ask potential customers to scan a QR code that goes to your email newsletter subscription page. You can create a free QR code in Google Chrome or Canva.

Other tips:

1. Stand if you are able and make eye contact. Try to make your body language welcoming. This means don't stand with your arms across your chest or leaning back and away from customers.

2. Have a quick line after you make eye contact that starts a conversation. I'm a big fan of, "What do you like to read?" I've also used, "Can I tempt you with some lesbian fiction?"

3. Don't make a face when people say, "I don't really read." There's a lot of people like that. Maybe they were born that way? It's okay.

4. Have the books standing up, not lying flat on the table. You can prop one copy up with the other copies you have, or you can buy stands for cheap at an office supply or dollar store.

5. Make it clear that you are the author, and you are selling your books. Readers can find that even more appealing than buying from any bookstore.

6. Have something to say besides "buy my book." People seem particularly interested in my writing process since I write with my wife, and I talk about that. (We're married. We talk to each other.) I give people directions when asked. If someone is looking for something I don't have, much like Santa Claus in the classic movie *Miracle on 34th Street*, I point them to other authors or vendors.

7. Don't assume who will and will not buy your book. I have a lot of men buy my lesbian fiction as presents for

their female friends, and I'm starting to get some gay male readers who really enjoy my work.

8. Find points of connection to start a conversation. A sincere compliment almost always works. Or talk about the weather. Ask if someone is local. Talk about the event. Small talk questions are your friends.

The goal is to engage people in some way. If they don't buy a book, maybe they'll sign up for your mailing list or take one of your cards and pass it on? Or maybe you'll have an interesting conversation with them? Maybe they'll say nice things about you to other people? Maybe they'll buy your book next year?

CHAPTER ELEVEN

Random marketing ideas that I like

Successful authors are all successful in their own ways and by their own definitions. If you publish one book and you're proud of it and you're done, that's okay. If you've published 50 books and you make $200 a month from your backlist a month, every month, that sounds like a great investment. Plenty of investment accounts don't do as well. There are poets who make a full-time living selling chapbooks at street fairs. There are lesbian authors who make a full-time living writing lesbian books. Some books sell. Others don't. Always keep your goals in mind. In this chapter, I'm going to talk about random marketing ideas that just didn't fit in the other chapters. Will they work for you? Maybe. They work for someone.

Swag

Who doesn't like swag? You go to some event, and some business gives you a tote bag that you use grocery shopping every week. Maybe they give you a magnet that lives on your refrigerator longer than the business actually exists? Like everything else, be stingy with your money and time. I have business cards printed with a book cover on one side and author contact information on the other. Those are very popular. We've also started creating refrigerator magnets. I would like to have shopping bags, so that when we sell books in person customers will end up walking around with their books in an Elizabeth Andre branded bag. This bag would then be used repeatedly until it wears out.

Then again, we once sold books in person at a lesbian event, and one of our customers wanted a bag. We didn't have one. The person ended up walking around with the books. We had some sales because she became our walking billboard.

Other popular choices include pens and bookmarks.

Blogging

I blog on Medium. This is primarily a way for me to publish my shorter writing and my opinions. I've published excerpts from my work, and sometimes original content. I publish in Prism and Pen, a Medium publication that has been good to me. I don't know how many sales this leads to, but I do enjoy it. There are so many blogging platforms. Pick one you like and go for it.

Subscriptions

There are authors who do quite well on subscription platforms like Patreon, Substack, and BuyMeACoffee which allow you to provide fans exclusive content in exchange for regular financial support. Ream is a newer service designed for authors. I haven't used them yet, but I am curious. I met the people behind this venture at a conference, and they have good energy. Ream may be in my future.

Crowdfunding

Kickstarter and Indiegogo are two of the main crowdfunding platforms, and I've seen authors use them successfully to raise money to produce special editions of their books. I launched an Indiegogo campaign in 2017 and raised nearly $1,900 for a photo shoot that would create diverse images for our book covers. Stock photo libraries didn't have great representation, and they still don't. I'm quite proud of this little campaign. It gave friends and family—who have long been supportive, but honestly our books are not for them and that's okay—an opportunity to support me financially, and they took the opportunity. I am forever grateful. However, the marketing was a lot of work. If you attempt to do this, have fun. I'm not sure I would do it again.

Reactive marketing

When the dust has settled and your beautifully written and edited book with the fabulous cover is making its way in the world, you can consider opportunities that present themselves, like public appearances or guest blogging. Have some fun with it. The sky's the limit, although always remember. It's rarely clear why one book sold and another didn't. As I write this, I just sold one copy of the *Curse of the Old Woods*, book 1 in my Paranormal Grievance Committee Chronicles series. This is a book I haven't promoted in years. Why did it sell? Not a clue.

PART II: THE NUTS AND BOLTS OF SELF-PUBLISHING LESBIAN FICTION

CHAPTER TWELVE

Navigating publishing platforms

Most publishing platforms will publish lesbian fiction. I'm not aware of any that won't publish any lesbian fiction at all, although some will not publish more explicit works. Also, lesbian fiction is more discoverable on some platforms than others. Each platform has its own advantages and disadvantages, and it is essential to choose those that best fit your goals.

Note about piracy: You can spend your time hunting down pirated copies of your e-book or audiobook, and you can pay services to scrub them from the internet. Or you can write more and spend your money promoting your books. The choice is yours. I don't spend a lot of time, if any at all, chasing down pirated copies of my books. It's a game of Whack-A-Mole that can suck up all your attention with minimal payoff. Yes, pirating is annoying. Yes, reading pirated books is theft and don't let anyone try to convince you otherwise. However, I have better things to do, like publishing lots of books. You can make different choices if you like.

So, let's publish a book.

Note: In the following chapters, I'm including the cover requirements for various platforms, but cover design is covered in Chapter Seven. You can have different covers for different editions, but this is rarely necessary. You will, however, need covers in different sizes. This is a minor thing that any designer should be able to handle. I will also include the technical requirements for blurbs and keywords and other metadata by platform. How to create engaging blurbs, choose effective keywords, and devise good metadata is covered in Chapter Eight about pull marketing.

Recommendation: There are a lot of platforms and a lot of choices. Don't do too much at once. It's okay to start slow. It's okay to publish on only one platform and expand. Or not. It's also okay to stay exactly where you are. It's okay to publish one book and call it a day. It's okay to publish 50 and keep going. It's okay for you to be you and do things your way.

And another recommendation: Most platforms have their own educational modules, webinars, and other opportunities. They are worth checking out, but always remember: They have been created by people looking to make money off you. This is not necessarily a bad agenda. We live in a capitalist society. Making money is a necessity, but it's always important to be aware of everyone's agendas, including your own.

CHAPTER THIRTEEN

Kindle Direct Publishing/Amazon (KDP)

What Kindle Direct Publishing (KDP) publishes: serialized fiction, e-books, paperbacks, and hardbacks
Where to start: https://kdp.amazon.com/

KDP is the behemoth of self-publishing. Many authors only publish on this platform, and the question of publishing exclusively on KDP versus publishing on multiple vendors (often referred to as "wide") is subject to endless debate among self-published authors.

Publishing an e-book exclusively on KDP allows it to be a part of the KDP Select program which means your book will be available in Kindle Unlimited (KU). KU readers pay a flat monthly fee for unlimited reading. When a KU reader reads your book, you are paid approximately a penny per two and a half pages. I know that doesn't sound like very much money, but it's a very popular program. KU readers read a lot, and the lesbian fiction bestseller lists on Amazon are dominated by books available through this program. Other perks of the KDP Select program include financial bonuses for popular books, higher royalty rates in some markets for book sales, and access to several exclusive marketing tools.

Should you do it? Maybe.

Reasons to publish exclusively on KDP:

- You only have to deal with one platform.
- KU money can be good.
- Exclusivity can give your book good visibility.
- It can be a particularly good choice for new authors.

Reasons to publish more widely:

- If you publish exclusively on KDP, you're putting all your eggs in one basket and beholden to one vendor. Every time Amazon makes a change, it may not be in your favor.
- Money can be good from other platforms as well.
- Not everyone buys their books from Amazon. For example, I sell a lot of books in the U.S. on Amazon, but I sell a lot of books in Canada on Kobo and a lot of books in South Africa on Google Play. I like serving lesbian readers around the world.
- Other platforms are not that hard.

I have published several books exclusively on KDP, but most are widely available. Personally, I'm not comfortable contributing to Amazon's increasing dominance in book publishing and selling, and I like serving all of my readers wherever they may be.

Ultimately, like many questions in the self-publishing world, it's your decision. KDP is certainly a great place to start self-publishing. It's better to start small and manageable and grow from there than to start big and get overwhelmed and exhausted before you've made much progress.

Remember: Kindle Select exclusivity only applies to e-books and doesn't last forever. You can still publish your paperback widely, and you can take your e-book out of the program after 90 days.

Let's walk through the steps of publishing on KDP.

Go to Kindle Direct Publishing. If you don't have an account with Amazon, you need to create one. It's okay to use the same account that you use for shopping on Amazon. It's not okay to set up multiple accounts on KDP, which is a common reason that Amazon may shut down an account.

There are four tabs on the top of the page, "Bookshelf," "Reports," "Community," and "Marketing." You should be on the "Bookshelf" tab. The "Reports" tab is where you will find your sales, and the "Community" tab will lead you to the support forum. "Marketing" will lead you to marketing tools. In the top right of the "Bookshelf" page is a large yellow button that says, "Create." Click that button. Choose whether to create a Kindle e-book, paperback, or hardcover. You will also have the option to create a series page or Kindle Vella, which was launched by Amazon in April 2021 and is one of KDP's newer offerings. I'm going to talk about it first, because if you don't publish on Vella first then you can't publish on Vella at all.

Should you publish on Vella? Maybe.

KDP: Serialized fiction

Kindle Vella is KDP's answer to serial reading apps like Radish. Readers read these stories one episode at a time in the Kindle app, and the first three episodes are always free. Readers buy packs of tokens which are redeemed for subsequent episodes. Episodes "cost" about one token per hundred words. Each episode is a maximum of 5,000 words.

Note: if you want to take a look at already published Kindle Vella stories, check if you have free tokens in your account. When I started publishing on Kindle Vella, I was surprised to find that I had 900 tokens available to me. I don't know where they came from. I didn't buy them, and I probably acquired them through Amazon's efforts to promote Kindle Vella.

There are a couple of different ways to approach

publishing on Kindle Vella. You can create a never-ending serialized story, posting a new episode at least once a week or more. Frequently updated stories tend to get more traction than those with long spaces between new episodes. You can also divide your already completed novel or novella into episodes. You can mark your Vella as "complete," so that readers know that what is published is all there is, and more episodes are not forthcoming.

Posting your novel or novella on Kindle Vella before publishing it as a full book has a couple of advantages. You can get some early reviews, and you can earn money from the program as people read episodes. Kindle Vella bonuses can be generous. I published my lesbian romantic comedy *My Favorite Wife* initially as a Vella. It has thus far earned about $2 in episode reads but over $45 in bonus money.

Note: You can only publish stories on Kindle Vella that have never been published anywhere else. You can then compile episodes into a book, but only one book. For example, because *My Favorite Wife* is on Vella, I can publish it as a novel, but I can't also include it in a boxed set with my other novels. You also need to wait 30 days after publishing on Vella before publishing your book of episodes. If I do want to include *My Favorite Wife* in a boxed set of my own books or someone else's, I would need to delete it from Vella. This involves deleting all the episodes and then the story itself from that platform.

To publish on Vella, go to your KDP bookshelf, click the big yellow "Create" button. Click the "Start a story" yellow button in the Kindle Vella box. Then click the teal "Start a story" button. The page that pops up next is headlined "Tell us about your story…" Enter your story title, author name, additional authors if you have them, your blurb (limit 500 characters), and a story image.

The story image is similar to a cover but doesn't have any text. It's just an image that relates to your story. This image should be square, in JPEG or TIFF format, no larger than 1,600 x 1,600 pixels, and no larger than two megabytes.

You can then select up to two browsing categories and seven story tags of 25 characters or fewer. You'll probably want to choose "Lesbian, Gay, Bisexual & Transgender Fiction" as your first category. Your second category should relate to your story's subgenre such as romance, erotica, or humor. Then click on "Publish and start episode 1" to start uploading your text.

Titles for individual episodes are optional, but I recommend having them. You can upload a Word file or cut and paste your text into a box on the page. Author notes are also optional, but I recommend writing them. Comment on the episode you've just uploaded. Foreshadow what is to come. I occasionally tell the stories behind the stories, meaning the real-life occurrence that inspired the story I wrote. You can also ask readers to follow you or give your episode a thumbs up. You can create an episode poll in order to gain more reader engagement. You can schedule your episodes. I like uploading all of my episodes and then setting them to publish one a day until the book is finished.

KDP: E-books

To publish an e-book on KDP, on your bookshelf page click the yellow "Create" button. On the next page click "Create e-book." You will be taken to a page that asks you the language of your book, the title, and the subtitle. Subtitles are optional, but I do like them. You can add your book to a series if you have created one. You can add an edition number. This can be important if you decide to republish a book with significant changes, but if this is your first version of your book, leave it blank. List your pen name (or real name) under author. Make sure you spell your name correctly. You can list contributors in the next box. You can list any co-authors or translators. You can also leave this box blank. Paste your blurb into the "Description" box, maximum 4,000 characters. Add bold, italics, or other basic formatting as desired. Click on "I own the copyright and I hold the necessary publishing rights."

The selection "This is a public domain work" is for books that have fallen out of copyright and are being republished such as *Frankenstein* by Mary Shelley or *Dracula* by Bram Stoker. Since this book is about self-publishing lesbian fiction, I won't be discussing public domain works very much. They are outside the scope of this book.

The next box asks about "Primary audience." If your book has sexually explicit images on the cover or inside the book or if the book's title contains sexually explicit language, select "yes." If it doesn't, select "no." You are required to answer that question, but the next one is optional. It asks about reading age. If you are writing children's or young adult books, you should select the appropriate ages for your book. This is the only way to get access to the children's and young adult categories. If you choose a minimum age, you must choose a maximum age. If you're writing books for adults, you can ignore this question.

The next drop-down menu asks about your primary marketplace. If you are in the U.S. or publishing from a country without a dedicated Amazon marketplace, you should probably choose Amazon.com. If you live outside the U.S. and your country has a dedicated Amazon marketplace, you should probably choose that marketplace.

The next drop-down menu asks you to choose categories for your books, and you are allowed three. I recommend being as specific as possible. To identify good categories for your book, look at a book similar to yours on Amazon. A book's categories are listed in the "Product details" section of the book's product page. You can click on the category to see the pathway to get to that category.

You can also use BkLNK to investigate categories of similar books. To use this website, identify a top selling book that has a similar audience to yours. Type in that book's ASIN number. The book's categories should pop up. Be aware that you will only be able to access some categories. Some categories are restricted to books placed in them by Amazon.

The most common categories for lesbian fiction e-books:

- LGBTQ+ e-books, Literature and fiction, Lesbian fiction
- LGBTQ+ e-books, Romance, Lesbian romance
- LGBTQ+ e-books, Erotica, Lesbian

I also put a lot of my books in Multicultural & interracial romance because that category fits. Your book may also have a non-lesbian specific category that works.

The next box asks you to input seven keywords, and this can be handled in several different ways. Generally, you want to combine keywords in the most logical order. Readers are more likely to search for "lesbian romance" than "romance lesbian." I brainstorm my keywords around setting, character types, character roles (strong female lead), plot themes, tropes, and story. I test my keywords by typing them into the Amazon search box on Amazon's home page to see what comes up. Amazon has an autocomplete function and will suggest additional keywords as you are typing yours in. I recommend doing this from an incognito web browser and consider including Amazon's suggestions.

You shouldn't include information covered elsewhere in your book's metadata, words already mentioned in your book categories, or subjective claims about quality.

Don't put "best novel ever" as one of your keywords no matter how much you believe that to be true.

Other terms to avoid include time-sensitive statements ("new," "on sale," "available now"), too obvious or generic terms ("book"), or any authors not connected to your book. You may think you're the next Rita Mae Brown, Radclyffe Hall, Ann Bannon, or Jae, but you can't include their names in your book's metadata. (You can include them as advertising terms. That will be addressed later.) Don't include Amazon program names like Kindle Unlimited or KDP Select or HTML tags. Each box allows for 50 characters.

The next choice you have to make is whether to release your book immediately or with a pre-order period of up to a year. I've played around with all sorts of pre-order period lengths. I'm not a fan of long pre-order periods. I prefer to either upload for immediate release or release in about four to five days. Long pre-orders can work if you have a large established fan base and someone else dedicated to marketing it for the entire pre-order period.

Reasons I don't like long pre-orders:

- Your Amazon rank moves up and down as if the book has already been published. If you don't have many sales in your pre-order period, your rank can become really low which makes sales once the book has been published less likely. A low rank makes your book less discoverable.
- Once you set up the pre-order, you now have a deadline for when you MUST have everything ready to upload and publish. If you miss this deadline, your book will be canceled, and you won't be able to do another pre-order on Amazon for a year.
- Marketing a book for that long a period of time is exhausting.

You are now at the end of the details page. You can click "Save draft" if you want to take a break and return to your book later or click "Save and continue" if you are ready to move along to the content page.

The first box asks you to upload a manuscript. You can upload a KPF (Kindle Packaging Format), EPUB, or DOCX file.

The DOCX file you can create in Microsoft Word, which is my preference. Creating an EPUB is also a good option. You can do that with Jutoh, Calibre, Apple Pages, Vellum, Scrivener, or several other programs. A KPF file can only be created using Kindle Create, a program that you can download for free on this page. Kindle Create does make good-looking e-books. However, you can only use the files it creates on KDP.

The formatting of an e-book is much as described in Chapter Six with the following exceptions:

- If using Microsoft Word, the table of contents needs to be set up by applying the "heading 1" style sheet to all chapter titles. You then need to click where you want to insert your table of contents. Go to the "References" tab and click "Table of Contents." Choose "Classic." Click "Table of Contents" again, but this time choose "Custom Table of Contents." In the dialog box that appears, clear the "Show Page Numbers" box. Set "Show Levels" to 1 and click "OK." When asked if you want to replace the table of contents, click "Yes."

- If you have other published books, you can hotlink to their Amazon pages in the front and back matter. I recommend using a universal link maker like BookLinker or Books2Read. These services will create links that automatically direct a reader to the Amazon site based in their country if there is one. The reason for this is you will probably have readers around the globe. For example, if a reader in Germany clicks a link that takes them to Amazon's U.S. store, they won't be able to buy your e-book there and will have to take extra steps to navigate to your book in Amazon's German store. Be nice to your readers. Don't make them work that hard.

You have the option of adding digital rights management (DRM) on this page. I recommend ignoring it. DRM is easy to break, annoys readers, and doesn't seem to do anything to stop piracy.

The next box asks you for a cover. KDP does have a built-in cover creator. If you have no budget, are just beginning in self-publishing, and don't have other options, go ahead and create your cover here, but the minute you have a few dollars you should create or buy a better one. The cover creator covers are basic and good enough, but you can do better. One of the many wonderful things about self-publishing, especially e-books, is that you can always update and improve things.

If you have your own cover created by a designer or by you, you can upload your JPG or TIFF file here. Your cover should ideally be 2,560 pixels in height and 1,600 pixels wide. It can be a minimum of 1,000 x 625 pixels but no more than 10,000 pixels. The ideal height/width ratio is at least 1.6:1. Dots per inch should be 72, and the cover image must be smaller than 50MB. Color profile should be RGB (red, green, blue). If your cover has a white or light color background, consider adding a 3- or 4-point wide frame around the image to make it stand out more on Amazon.

For those unfamiliar with printing measurements, there are 12 points to a pica, approximately 6 picas to an inch.

The content of the cover image must not infringe another publisher's or artist's copyright. It also can't mention pricing or other temporary promotional offers.

The next box asks you about AI-generated content. If you used AI tools in creating texts, images, and/or translations in your book, answer, "yes." If you didn't, respond, "no."

The next box allows you to preview your e-book as it will look on several different devices. You can view your book within your web browser or download it. I always view it within my browser.

The next box asks for an ISBN and a publisher name. Both are optional. Whether to buy your own ISBNs or use those provided by various publishing platforms is a matter of ongoing debate in the self-publishing community. I don't buy my own ISBNs and haven't found a compelling reason to do so yet. I do have a publisher name. You don't have to.

You are now at the end of the content page. You can click "Save as Draft" if you want to take a break and return to your book later or click "Save and Continue" if you are ready to move along to the pricing page.

The first box on the pricing page asks whether you want to enroll your e-book in KDP Select. If you choose to enroll in this program, your e-book will be exclusive to KDP for 90 days and cannot be published elsewhere, although you can publish your paperback on other platforms.

The next box asks you about the territories for which you hold distribution rights for your book. Unless you have sold the rights to your book in certain countries, select "all territories, (worldwide rights)."

The next box asks for your primary marketplace. If you live in the U.S. or in a country without a dedicated Amazon marketplace, choose Amazon.com. If you live in a country with a dedicated Amazon marketplace, choose that.

The next box asks you to select your royalty plan and set your prices. For the 35% royalty rate, you can set your U.S. prices from $0.99 to $200. To get 70%, your e-book must be priced $2.99 to $9.99.

Notes about prices:

- Because of KDP's royalty structure, I price most of my books between $2.99 and $9.99.

- I do have some books at 99 cents. These are loss leaders that are usually short stories, although I do sometimes mark down my more expensive books to $0.99 for special sales.

- I have grouped some of my books into large boxed sets that are priced at more than $9.99. Because of KDP's royalty structure, I don't publish those e-books on KDP. I do publish them on other platforms.

- Your price on KDP can be lower than other platforms, but it can't be higher. If it is, KDP may price match and lower the price of your book, regardless of what you input.

- Even though you have input your price into KDP, Amazon may choose to discount it. You may be able to get any pricing differences fixed by contacting KDP.

To contact KDP, you need to use the very tiny "contact us" button on the very bottom of the page.

When you have input your prices, you can click either "Save as Draft" or "Publish your Kindle e-book." If you click "Publish" (and I hope you do), you should get a "Congratulations!" pop up that asks whether you want to publish your e-book as a paperback. If you do, and you're ready to do so, click "Start Your Paperback Now." If you don't want to publish a paperback or you're not ready to do so, click "Close."

Unless you've set up a pre-order, your e-book will be available on Amazon in less than 72 hours. Congratulations! You are now a published author.

You can make changes to your book any time after your book has finished its review period. Your book will be marked "in review" and locked immediately after you upload it. If you have a preorder period, it will be locked 72 hours before your book is published. To make changes, on the right-hand side of the book listing on the bookshelf page, click the three dots. The pop-up menu will allow you to return to the details, content, and pricing pages. You can also edit your KDP Select enrollment. Make your changes and resubmit. It will be once again locked and in review for up to 72 hours, so you will want to make all your changes at once, if possible.

KDP: Paperbacks

There are a few ways to start the process of publishing your paperback, and they all lead to the paperback details page.

- If you published your e-book and responded that you wanted to start your paperback now, you will be taken directly to the paperback details page. It will be linked to your e-book page and pre-populated with a lot of information from the e-book.

- If you didn't, here's how to start your paperback. If your e-book is published it will appear on your bookshelf with buttons that ask you to create a paperback or link an existing one. If you have an existing paperback version of your book published on Amazon, you can link to it. If you don't (the more likely situation) here's how to publish your paperback and have it linked to your e-book.
- If you want to start a paperback from scratch without an e-book already published, go to your bookshelf page and click the large yellow "Create" button. On the next page, you can click "Create paperback." The paperback details page is exactly the same as the e-book details page.

Once on the paperback details page, choose your book's primary language and input the title and subtitle. You can add details about the series, if the book is part of one, and add the edition number if it isn't the first published version of your book. On this page, you also input the primary author, other contributors, and description (blurb). This page also asks whether your book contains adult-only content, the reading age of the primary audience, primary marketplace, categories, and keywords. If your book is a low-content book like a coloring book or journal or a large print book, meaning that it is in at least 16-point type, you can indicate that here. Lastly, you can add your keywords. Click "Save as Draft" if you want to take a break and return to it later or click "Save and Continue" to move on to the "Content" page.

On the "Content" page you can input an ISBN that you purchased or choose to utilize a free ISBN from Amazon. I use the free ISBNs. I know many authors like to buy their own.

Note: Whatever you decide about your ISBN, make sure you add the number to your paperback's front matter.

You can set the publication date, but unfortunately you

can't set up a pre-order for a paperback. That's only for e-books. If you chose a date in the future, your book will appear on Amazon on that date, but, unlike an e-book pre-order, the book will not be visible and readers will not be able to order it until the actual publication date. Choose your ink and paper type. I usually go with a black and white interior with white paper, although cream would probably look nice as well. If your book has a lot of illustrations, you may want to go with a color interior. For trim size, I usually choose 6"x9", but some authors prefer 5"x8" or 5.5"x8.5". Like so much in self–publishing, there isn't one right answer, although you probably want to pick a size and stick with it. Readers like it when their paper books from one author are all the same size, so they look good on a bookshelf. I usually choose "no bleed" and a matte cover. Glossy is also an option.

All about bleed: No blood involved. I promise. This is a printing term and refers to text or artwork that extends beyond the edge of where the printed page will be trimmed to size. There has to be some wiggle room in where a page will be trimmed because that knife will never cut perfectly. Generally speaking, the bleed will include a "red zone," which means it will definitely be cut off and a "yellow zone." No critical information should be included in the yellow zone, but some of it may still appear in the finished product, so it still needs to look good.

Your next step is to upload your manuscript. KDP recommends uploading a PDF, which can be created from the formatted Word file you made earlier (see Chapter Six). I recommend a PDF as well. You can upload a DOC, DOCX, HTML, or RTF file. I tried uploading a DOCX file when I first started publishing paperbacks, and it did not look good. Convert your file to a PDF and upload that. You'll avoid a lot of heartache.

The next box asks you to upload a cover. You can use KDP's built-in cover creator if you don't have your cover already made by yourself or someone else.

With an e-book, the cover is one size no matter how many pages your book is. With a paperback, size matters, and in addition to a front cover, you need a spine and a back cover. I recommend using KDP's print cover calculator to figure out the dimensions and create a template. You or your designer can then use this template to create the cover. The spine should include the author name and book title, unless the book is shorter than 120 pages. Then the spine will be too small for that information. Your spine on a book that short will be blank. I put the blurb on the back cover. If I have any glowing reviews, I may add a few words from one of them. Don't forget to leave space for the barcode.

The next box asks you about AI-generated content. If you used AI tools in creating texts, images, and/or translations in your book, answer, "yes." If you didn't, respond, "no."

The next box gives you the opportunity to preview your book. You should definitely take this opportunity. KDP may also alert you to problems that need or should be fixed before printing.

Note: While nearly every detail of an e-book's metadata and content can be changed after publication. You cannot change the language, book title, subtitle, edition number, primary author, ink, paper type, and trim size of a paperback. Also, while terms such as "boxed set" can be used on an e-book, they can't be used on a paperback.

You are at the bottom of the page once more. Click "Save as Draft" if you are taking a break or "Save and Continue" to move onto the paperback rights and pricing page. The first box asks you about territories. You can choose to publish your book worldwide or only in certain territories. The next box asks you your primary marketplace, and the next box asks about pricing, royalty, and distribution.

I set my paperback prices to end in .95. You can base all of your prices on the Amazon.com marketplace or round the numbers to make most of them end in .95. You get 60% of the cover price if someone purchases the paperback directly from an Amazon marketplace. You get 40% if someone purchases your book from a marketplace included in Amazon's "expanded distribution" option, which is available only on Amazon's U.S. and U.K. platforms. Expanded distribution means your paperback will be distributed through Barnes & Noble's online bookstore and Waterstones' online bookstore. Other bookstores will also have the option of ordering it. It sounds like a great idea, and I use KDP's expanded distribution for most of my books. You may not, however, want to use it if one of your goals is to get your book into brick-and-mortar bookstores. IngramSpark is more useful for that, and I discuss that vendor and brick-and-mortar bookstores in Chapter Twenty.

At the bottom of the page, you can request a proof. This will cost you a few dollars plus shipping, and it's worth doing.

After all that, you can click "Save as Draft" if you are still waiting on your proof or are not quite ready to publish. If you're ready, click "Publish Your Paperback Book."

Your book can take up to 72 hours to publish, and then congratulations! You are a published author, and you rock.

You can make changes any time after your book has finished its review period. Your book will be marked "In review" and locked immediately after you upload it. To make changes, on the right-hand side of the book listing on the bookshelf page, click the three dots. The pop-up menu will allow you to return to the details, content, and pricing pages. Make your changes and resubmit. It will once again be locked and in review for up to 72 hours, so you want to make all your changes at once, if possible.

KDP: Hardcover

KDP started publishing hardcover books in 2021. This program is still in beta. I have uploaded some of my books as hardcovers, but I haven't sold any. I'm not saying you shouldn't have your books available as hardcovers. I am saying that doing so should be a lower priority than getting your e-books and paperbacks published.

Starting a hardcover is much like starting a paperback. You click on the yellow "Create" button at the top of your bookshelf page or click "Create hardcover" under an existing e-book and/or paperback listing.

The hardcover details page is very similar to the paperback and e-book details page and if you have already published those versions of your book, this page will be pre-populated. The hardcover content page is also similar to the paperback content page.

Note: You will need a unique ISBN that is different from the one for the paperback version of your book, but the interior is otherwise the same. The big difference between a paperback and a hard cover is the cover size and cover layout. You will need to go to KDP's print cover calculator to figure out the dimensions and create a hardcover template. Expanded distribution is not available for hardcovers, but the rights and pricing page is otherwise the same as the paperback rights and pricing page.

Also Note: While nearly every detail of an e-book's metadata and content can be changed after publication. You cannot change the language, book title, subtitle, edition number, primary author, ink, paper type, or trim size for a hardcover. Also, while terms such as "boxed set" can be used on an e-book, they can't be used on a hardcover.

Note: You can make changes to your book any time after your book has finished its review period. Your book will be marked "In review" and locked immediately after you upload it. To make changes, click the three dots on the right-hand side of the book listing on the bookshelf page. The pop-up menu will allow you to return to the details, content, and pricing pages. Make your changes and resubmit. It will once again be locked and in review for up to 72 hours, so you want to make all your changes at once, if possible.

KDP: Marketing

KDP has several built-in marketing tools that can be quite effective, including the opportunity to create a dedicated author page for your pen name.

You must already have at least one book published on Amazon to qualify for an author page. Go to Amazon Author Central and click "Join for Free." Sign in using the same login credentials that you used for your KDP account. Read the terms and conditions and click "Accept." Enter your author name or book title into the search field. A list of possible books will appear. Select your book to create the account. Amazon will send you a confirmation email to finish creating the account.

You can have up to three pen names on your author central account,

After your account is verified and your author page has been created, readers will be able to follow you, and you will be able to track how many followers you have after you have more than 20. You won't know who these people are, and you won't be able to contact them directly. However, if your followers allow marketing emails from Amazon.com, they will be notified within 60 days of your book's release or the availability of a pre-order. This is a great example of passive marketing. Amazon takes care of it, but you have no control over it. It can lead to sales.

You can also make book recommendations to your followers. These are books you've read by other authors that you think your readers would like. I haven't used this feature. If you do, I'd be curious to hear if it helps your sales.

On your author profile page, you can add a photo and your biography in English, French, German, and other languages. If you don't want to add a photo of yourself, you can use a book cover, which is what I do. Biographies should be a thousand characters or fewer.

Should you translate your biography to other languages? If you have translated your books to other languages, absolutely. If you haven't, then no.

Note: Translating my books into other languages is on my long list of things I want to do with my stories, and I think it's a great idea. I won't be discussing translations in this book because I have no experience with them. I will say that unless you are a fluent writer in a second language, you should hire a professional for this kind of work.

On your book's listing in Author Central you can add brief excerpts from editorial reviews. These are reviews that your book has received from newspapers, magazines, or blogs. Pick out one or two of the best sentences and don't go over 3,000 characters. You can also add notes from the author.

Your Amazon Author page is a convenient place, if you have more than one book published, to look at them all in one place. You can view your books' sales ranks and reviews on the various Amazon marketplaces.

Other KDP marketing opportunities include being able to create X-ray information, a series page (if your book is part of a series), A+ content, advertisements, and price promotions.

X-ray can be accessed from the three-dot drop-down menu on the right-hand side of your book listing on the bookshelf. It allows you to provide additional information about characters, places, and terms used in your book. To add X-ray, click "Add X-ray" on the three-dot drop down menu. This will take you to your book's X-ray page. You will then get an alert that says, "X-ray content has not been enabled for this book." Click the "Request X-ray" yellow button. You will then get a notice saying that generating X-ray content will take up to 30 minutes and that you will receive an email when it is ready. I've never waited more than a minute, but once you get that email go back to the three-dot drop down menu. It should now read, "Launch X-ray." You will then be presented with a brief tutorial about how X-ray works. Custom descriptions are required for all characters or made-up place names. You can choose a Wikipedia entry for things that are real such as the city of Chicago or the Moon. You can exclude terms that you don't want to add additional info to. I try to give brief descriptions of my characters without providing any spoilers. If something or someone is only mentioned once or twice, I don't write special X-ray information for it. When you are finished or just want to take a break, you can click "Review and publish X-ray" in the upper right-hand corner. Your X-ray content will be locked while it is being reviewed, but I've never experienced a review of longer than a few minutes.

This process can be time consuming, but Amazon says readers like X-ray content. I have never heard any complaints either way, nor have any readers requested it. That said, when I have the time, I create X-ray content for my books.

If your book is part of a series, you can manage a series page. Make sure you list a series title in your metadata when you publish your book, and make sure the series title is exactly the same from book to book. This action creates the series page. To manage the series page, go to the three-dot menu and click "manage series." From the series page, you can add existing titles, create new titles, add a series description, and edit the book order. You can also "Edit series relationship." This is important because while most books in a series are a fairly straightforward 1, 2, 3, etc. and considered "main content," you may want to have "related content" such as a boxed set or a prequel.

The other marketing programs can be accessed by

clicking on "Promote and advertise," either on the three-dot drop-down menu or on the "Promote and advertise" button that is next to your book on the bookshelf page. From the top box on the "Promote your book on Amazon" page, you can manage the KDP Select enrollment. This can include enrolling your book in this program or tracking the date when you can end your participation and publish your book more widely. Every 90 days you have the option of taking your book out of the program. If your book is enrolled and you do nothing, your enrollment will renew ad infinitum. Once you take it out, you can put it back in if you want to, although if you've gone ahead and published widely make sure all the non-Amazon copies of your e-book are removed from sale. KDP Select requires exclusivity for e-books.

If your book is enrolled in KDP Select, the next box will give you the option of running a price promotion. These price promotions are only for KDP Select enrolled books, and you can participate in one price promotion during each 90-day period. Your options are a Kindle Countdown Deal or Free Book Promotion. You can use one or the other, but not both.

You can set up a Kindle Countdown Deal to discount your book on Amazon.com and Amazon.co.uk for a set period of time. The Free Book Promotion allows you to give your book away on all Amazon marketplaces for up to five days. You can run these days consecutively or scatter them over the 90-day period. While you can only use one of these promotions in a 90-day period, you can choose one type of promotion in one 90-day period and choose another for the next 90-day period.

From this page, you can also set up an Amazon ad campaign, an option for all books published on Amazon whether they are in KDP Select or not. These are cost-per-click (CPC) ads, which means you bid on the chance for a click. If your bid is the highest, your ad is the one that will be shown to a potential reader. You get charged when a reader clicks your ad.

Note: You can also access Amazon ads directly and sign on using your Amazon credentials.

From your marketing and promotions page, choose your marketplace and then click the yellow button, "Create an ad campaign." This will take you to a screen where you are offered three types of ads. You want "Sponsored Products." You can ignore "Sponsored Brands" and "Lockscreen Ads."

You know when you search for something on Amazon, and the result is a bunch of listings? The ones marked "sponsored" are ads that have been paid for.

After you've clicked on "Sponsored Products," you will be taken to a page where you can create your ad. Choose "Custom text ad" if you want to add text to your ad. Choose "Standard ad" if you don't want to add your own text. You can then choose the product you want to advertise.

Note: Not all books can be advertised. My spicier books cannot. Amazon also doesn't allow me to advertise the book my dad wrote about Jesus. Make sure you read their terms and conditions to learn what Amazon will allow you to advertise and what it won't.

You can choose automatic or manual targeting as well as default bids. Automatic targeting is a good choice to make an ad very quickly, but that also means the metadata you used to publish your book has to be spot on. That's the information Amazon will use to create your automatic ad.

Choosing manual targeting allows you to customize the keywords, products, and categories that may trigger an ad for your book.

Note: You are not looking to advertise to everybody. You are looking to advertise to the people most likely to buy your book. Hence, "book" is a surprisingly expensive keyword but not a good one.

For manual targeting, spend some time brainstorming your keywords. Start with your own titles and your pen name and work from there. Try to make your keywords as specific as possible. Sources for keywords include the "Also boughts" on your book's page. "Instant data scraper," a free Google Chrome plug-in has also been recommended. Many authors use Publisher Rocket to identify good keywords.

If you are manually targeting your ad, when you select a keyword you can choose, "broad," "phrase," or "exact." I recommend using "broad." Use your judgment as to whether to add or ignore a keyword that Amazon has suggested for your book. You can then click on "Enter list" to add your own keywords. You can also upload a spreadsheet file with your keywords.

You can set "negative keyword targeting" or "negative product targeting." This means that if someone types in certain keywords or looks at certain products, your book will NOT be shown. Negative keywords can be important to avoid wasting money on someone who is unlikely to buy your book. For example, for my books in the *Paranormal Grievance Committee Chronicles* series, I use "romance" as a negative keyword. Lesbian romance is very popular, but there's minimal romance in this series. Readers looking for romance are unlikely to buy any books in this series, and if they do, they may be disappointed.

Unless you choose "Standard ad," the next box asks you for custom text, and the next box will show you a preview of your ad. After that, you can set your campaign bidding strategy. I recommend selecting "Dynamic bids - down only."

At the bottom of the page is a "settings" box. Here you can name your campaign, add your campaign to a portfolio, set a start and end date, and set a daily budget. I recommend $1-$5 a day and low bids.

Note: Your campaign may now spend up to 100% more than your daily budget using unspent amounts from previous days in the month. Pay attention to this because it can be particularly startling on high traffic days such as Amazon Prime days.

You can now save your campaign as a draft or launch it.

Once you have set up at least one campaign, you will be able to view them on the "Campaign manager" page. This page will provide your spend, sales, and average cost of sale (ACOS). This will be presented as raw numbers and as a graph. Scroll down and you'll be able to see, by campaign, whether the campaign is active or not, the name of the campaign, campaign type, start date, end date, daily budget, cost type, spend, orders, sales, Kindle Unlimited page reads, and several other numbers.

Note: Amazon has free webinars and training courses on their advertising program, and they are worth checking out. Bryan Cohen also has a very popular (and free) five-day ad challenge that he runs several times a year. There are numerous paid courses. The ones I regularly hear good things about, although I haven't taken them, are Bryan Cohen's paid Ad School course that follows his free five-day ad challenge and Mark Dawson's Ads For Authors course.

Also note: Always keep in mind that Amazon's agenda is to make the most amount of money for itself and its shareholders. Your agenda should be to make money or at least keep as much of your own money as possible. Always remember that while you may work with an organization and find benefit, that organization can have its own agenda.

If this all seems too complicated or you just don't want to run ads yourself, you can hire someone or a company to do it for you such as Written Word Media, which can handle Facebook and Amazon ads with their Reader Reach program.

Also on the promotion page is the opportunity to create A+ content. This consists of images, text, and comparison tables that you can add to your Amazon detail page to provide more information to readers as they consider buying your book. For some of my books, I've created a very simple graphic and pull quote. For others, like my *Lesbian Light Reads* series, I've created tables comparing the various volumes.

Note: If you want A+ content on all marketplaces, you must create it for each marketplace. The various marketplaces do not share A+ content.

Also note: There are two additional choices on the three-dot menu that you should understand. "Unpublish" does exactly that. Your book will be removed from Amazon marketplaces. You can also "archive" a title. This does not change anything about its published status on Amazon, but it does remove the listing from your bookshelf. This can be particularly handy if you have a lot of titles and don't want to wade through listings that don't need your attention.

CHAPTER FOURTEEN

Rakuten Kobo

What Kobo publishes: e-books and audiobooks
Where to start:
https://www.kobo.com/us/en/p/writinglife

You can publish e-books and audiobooks on Kobo, and I'm a big fan of their publishing platform, which is clean and easy to use. Books published on Kobo are distributed to at least 26 vendors in 15 countries.

You can also access Kobo through an aggregator such as Draft2Digital/Smashwords. I did that for a long time. It's very common for authors who publish wide to self-publish on KDP and then use an aggregator for all other platforms. If you decide to expand the number of platforms upon which you publish directly, Kobo is a good first choice.

Reasons to publish directly on Kobo:

- Access to its promotional program
- Slightly higher royalties than what you would get through an aggregator
- A greater degree of control

- Access to vetted third-party sellers of publishing services such as cover design
- Kobo's parent company, Rakuten, has a deal with Walmart, and your e-book will be for sale on that large retailer's website.

Reasons to publish on Kobo through an aggregator:

- It's additional work to publish directly on multiple platforms.
- The minimum to get a royalty payment from Kobo is $50 (Canadian), so it may take you a while to get any money.

Let's walk through the steps of publishing on Kobo.

Go to Kobo Writing Life. Create your account. You can use the same sign-on credentials you use for Walmart.com or create an account linked to your email, Facebook, Google, or Apple account. You will then be taken to a page that will ask for your name (required), address (required) and your publisher name (optional). You can set your email preferences. I recommend getting their Writing Life newsletter. It's a good one. You also need to accept their terms of service. I recommend reading them. You will then be sent an email to confirm your account.

After you confirm your account, add your payment details so you can get paid. You will then be taken to the main page. At the top are drop down menus for "My Account" which includes payment information, contact information, terms of service, an option to change the language of the page, a link to the Kobo store, a link to Kobo's writing blog (worth checking out), and a "Sign Out" button.

The next row includes tabs for a "Dashboard" where you can see your sales; "E-books" where you can start the process to publish your e-book; "Author services" which can guide you to vetted editors, cover designers, translators and other publishing professionals; and "Help," which has lots of resources for novice and experienced publishers alike.

You can then start publishing an e-book.

Kobo: E-books

From the e-books tab, you should see a red button that reads "Create new e-book." After you click that button, you will be taken to the "Describe your e-book page." Required fields include "E-book title" and "Author." Optional fields include "E-book subtitle," "Series name," "Publisher name," and "Imprint." This page also asks if this is the first time you are publishing this book. If the answer is "no," you will then be asked for the original publication date. This is also the page where you upload your cover, which should be 1,600 x 2,400 pixels, with a 2:3 aspect ratio. The cover file should be no larger than 5MB and a JPG or PNG file. This page also asks you for your ISBN.

Note: You cannot use a free ISBN from another vendor such as Smashwords. You can buy your own, but an ISBN is optional. I leave this field blank. Other questions on this page include the book's main language and whether it is in the public domain. If you wrote this book, it is not in the public domain.

You can also choose up to three categories for your book on this page. Fiction & Literature, LGBT, Lesbian; Romance, Erotica, Lesbian; and Romance, LGBT, Lesbian are the specifically lesbian categories. Do not hesitate to add categories that are not specifically lesbian if that is appropriate for your book.

The final box on this page asks for your synopsis (blurb). Kobo does not have an option to add keywords.

At the end of the page, you can hit "Save and continue," which will take you to the "Add e-book content page" or "Save and return to the library," which saves your book as draft.

On the "Add e-book content" page, you can upload your

book in EPUB, DOC, DOCX, MOBI, or ODT formats. I've had a good experience uploading as a DOCX and having Kobo convert it to an EPUB. I upload a DOCX file formatted as described in Chapter Six. After Kobo has finished processing the file, you can download and preview your e-book, which I recommend as a quality control step. At the bottom of the page, you will see "Validation results," which will tell you the issues that either must be fixed as well as those that don't have to be, but it would be nice if you would.

Note: Make sure your book doesn't mention or have links to other vendors. You can include links to your website, social media, email newsletter, or other books already published on Kobo. If you do have other books published on Kobo, make it a global link, not just the one that goes to the U.S. store. In order to do that, you can copy the link to your book, but remove any references to country or language from the link. Make sure the edited link works.

The next page is focused on "Rights and distribution." You have the option of applying "Digital rights management." I don't bother. It's not an effective way to prevent piracy and can just annoy your readers. You also have the option of selecting worldwide distribution or picking and choosing which countries in which your book is sold.

The next box is particularly interesting. You can decide whether to participate in Kobo Plus and if you want your books distributed to Overdrive. Kobo Plus is a subscription reading program like Kindle Unlimited, but exclusivity is not required. Authors are paid based on the number of minutes readers spend reading their books. I have all my books in Kobo Plus, and I see no reason not to participate in this program.

Overdrive distributes to libraries, and I set my price two to three times the retail price because I was advised by a Kobo representative to do so.

Interesting lesson learned: When I increased my library prices, not only did the money I earned per sale go up but the number of sales I had to libraries increased. Higher prices can make people feel like they're getting something of higher quality and can make your book more appealing.

The next page asks you to set your price. Books priced $1.99 to $12.99 are paid at a 70% royalty rate. Books priced lower or higher than that pay out at a 45% royalty rate. You can also schedule a sale. This is a nice feature because you can set it and forget it. If you're setting up a sale for a particular time on other platforms, you usually have to remember to do so just before your sale starts. Then you have to remember to change the price again once the sale is over.

The next page is where you hit "Publish," and you can choose to publish immediately or set up a pre-order.

Kobo: Audiobooks

Note: To start publishing audiobooks, you need to send a request to do so through the "Contact us" button at the bottom of the webpage.

Once Kobo has given you the "Audiobook" tab, click on it. Similar to the e-book page, there will be a red button that says "Create new audiobook." On the next page you can input your title, subtitle, series information, contributors, synopsis, publisher name, imprint, publication date, and release date. The release date can be in the future if you want to set up a pre-order. The next box asks for an ISBN, and you can use one you've purchased or a free one from Kobo. The next boxes ask you to select a language and whether the book is abridged or unabridged. You can then select up to three categories. Most lesbian books fall into fiction and literature-LGBT-lesbian, romance-erotica-lesbian, and/or romance-LGBT-lesbian. Other categories may be appropriate.

The next section asks you to upload a cover image. It must be square; a PNG, JPG, or JPEG; no larger than 5MB; and no smaller than 600 x 600 pixels. If your cover image is not square it will be converted to a square. I don't know what that would look like, but you're probably better off uploading your own already square cover image.

The next box asks you to upload a sample, and this is recommended. Only MP3 and M4A audio formats are allowed, and the file should not exceed 200MB. Do not include explicit material and try to avoid any spoilers.

The next box is where you will upload the actual audio files for your book. Once again, only MP3 and M4A audio formats are acceptable, although Kobo will publish human- and AI-narrated audiobooks. Individual files must be less than 200MB each, and the total size of all files combined must be less than 2GB. After your audio files are uploaded, Kobo will create a table of contents. Make sure things are in the right order.

The next boxes allow you to select your geographic rights (world or by country), enroll your book in Kobo Plus (which I recommend), and set your price. Books that are less than $2.99 in U.S. dollars receive a 35% royalty. Higher priced books get 45%.

You can then hit the publish button or save a draft of your information to publish later.

Kobo: Marketing

Note: To get access to Kobo's built in promotion opportunities, send a message through the contact button.

I've landed quite a few of the promo opportunities that I've applied for on Kobo, and most of them are free to participate. I know many self-published authors have found success with them.

Alas, I have not, and I haven't heard good things about

Kobo promos from other lesbian fiction authors. I'm not saying you shouldn't try them. I just hope you have better luck than I have had.

CHAPTER FIFTEEN

Google Play

What Google Play publishes: e-books and audiobooks
Where to start:
https://play.google.com/books/publish/u/0/

Google Play, an online store where people can purchase apps, games, music, movies, and books, has gone through all sorts of ups and downs. I've attempted to publish on this platform a couple of times over the years, but up until about 2020 I wouldn't have recommended anyone else to do so for all sorts of reasons.

But enough about the past. The Google Play platform of the present is much easier to access and publish on, and they have access to a huge market. I like their current iteration, and I'm enjoying publishing on them.

You can access them through PublishDrive, an aggregator with access to numerous publishing platforms, or direct. I will talk more about PublishDrive and other aggregators in Chapter Eighteen. In this chapter I go through the steps of publishing directly.

You will need a Google account. After you have set that

up if you didn't already have one, your first step is to visit the Google Play Books Partner Center and create a publisher account. The first screen asks you if you are a publisher, self-published author, or distributor or service provider. If you are only publishing your own books, select "Self-published author."

The next screen asks for your publisher name, which can be your pen name, and your country. This should be the country where your primary bank is located and where you will receive payments. This screen also asks for your website (optional) and your phone number (required). The next screen asks you what emails you want to receive from the Google Play Books Partner Center and to agree to Google's terms and conditions. You will then be taken to a page where you can create a payment profile, fill out some tax information, and start adding your first book. Your options are "Sell e-book on Google Play," and create an "Auto-narrated audiobook." I go through the steps for both of those options in the next two sections.

You can also choose "Offer a preview on Google Books." If your book is published on Google Play, a preview on Google Books, a comprehensive index of all books, is created automatically. If you are not published on Google Play, this is a way for you to upload a preview on Google Books. An author may want to do that as a way of promoting their book for sale on other platforms.

Google Play: E-books

To publish your e-book, sign into the Google Play Partner Center. Click on the "Book catalog" tab on the left-hand side of the page. At the top of the page, there will be a blue button, "Add book." You can ignore most of the options under the "advanced options" button. From the drop-down menu on the next page select "Sell e-book on Google Play." Another drop-down menu will appear, "Select book ID." I use the Google Book ID (GGKey), but you can use an ISBN or EAN number if you have one. Click "Save and continue."

The next few pages ask you about the book including title, subtitle, and description. Google does not give you the option of adding keywords. Rather, in the description box you should paste your blurb followed by quotes from reviews and a block of text that includes your keywords.

Note: This keyword block has long been a part of publishing on Google Play, although there are indications that this may no longer be preferred.

The following boxes ask for language, publisher name, publication date, and the on-sale date. Choosing an upcoming on-sale date allows you to set up a pre-order period. Then select e-book under format and input your approximate number of pages. The next boxes ask you for a minimum and maximum reader age and whether the book is for mature audiences. You can add related books such as paperback and hardcover editions by other publishers.

Hit "Save and continue" to move on to the next page, which will ask you about genres. If you are in the U.S., you will use BISAC categories. The ones for lesbian fiction include:

Fiction/Erotica/LGBTQ+/Lesbian;

Fiction/LGBTQ+/Lesbian; and

Fiction/Romance/LGBTQ+/Lesbian.

Don't hesitate to choose non-lesbian categories if they are appropriate.

"Save and Continue" will take you to the contributors page. Here you can add your pen name and your pen name's biography.

The next page allows you to create a series, and the page after that includes lots of settings that impact how your book shows up on Google Play and Google Books such as whether to have digital rights management (DRM) encryption, the amount of text to preview, and the amount of text that can be copied. Google Play doesn't recommend DRM but does recommend that the other two values be set to 20%. I follow those recommendations.

Clicking on an arrow on this page will take you to "Advanced settings" that affect the PDF and EPUB versions of your book as well as how your book appears on Google Books. Once again, I mostly follow Google's recommendations.

The next page is the content page. Unlike several publishing platforms, you can't upload a Word or text document to be converted to an EPUB, PDF, or other book format. You have to make these files yourself. Google Play also has file naming conventions that need to be followed. I use Apple's Pages app to turn my previously formatted Microsoft Word doc into an EPUB and PDF, and there are numerous other apps that will convert a Word document into an EPUB and PDF. I make sure any links direct readers to my other books in the Google Play store.

File names can just be the Google book number or ISBN. If your pdf does not include a cover, this should be followed by an underscore and "interior" for the book content or "front cover" for the book's cover. Cover files should be a PNG, JPG, JPEG, TIF, TIFF, or PDF. Cover files must have a minimum resolution of 640 pixels. The maximum height and width are 7,200 pixels.

All files should be smaller than 2GB.

After your book is published, you can add "Content reviewers." These are people who you want to receive your book at no charge. Maybe they've agreed to review the book? Maybe they're people you want to check out your book set up. This is one of my favorite features on Google Play because it is super easy. All you have to do is add the person's email address.

You can set your prices on the next page. I recommend setting the price and then selecting "no" for the question as to whether tax is included. You can set one price and allow Google to make currency conversions automatically or set prices by country. The effective prices will appear in the box below. Google pays 70% royalty rates on e-books sold in more than 60 countries.

The next page asks you to review what you have input. You can then hit "Publish."

Google Play: Audiobooks

The main reason I started publishing on Google Play after a couple of false starts was to get access to their AI-narrated audiobook program. I'd been wanting to create audio versions of my books for years but had always found the process daunting. This felt like a good entry point. Not only is their AI audio program free, but as long as your book remains on sale at Google Play you can sell your AI-narrated audiobook files on other platforms that allow AI-narrated audiobooks, such as Kobo.

After you have uploaded your e-book, go to the book catalog tab and click the "Add book" button. From the "Sell option" drop down menu, choose "Create an auto-narrated audiobook." The next drop-down menu will ask you to "Select an e-book to auto-narrate." This book must be available in EPUB format and for sale on the Google Play platform. The following drop-down menu will ask you for an ISBN/EAN or offer you a Google Book ID. You can then click "Save and continue." Translating your EPUB into an audiobook may take a few minutes, depending on how long it is.

Once your audiobook is ready, you should edit the audio file. This can be time-consuming, but it is worth the time. You can add and remove text. (**Note:** this will not affect your original EPUB file.) You can also choose a default narrator (upper left of screen), adjust narrator speed, and edit pronunciation. In addition to a default narrator for most of your text, on the right side of the top of the screen you can choose particular voices for some of the characters or types of characters. Your choice of narrators is limited, although Google has promised more choices are coming. Currently available accents include American, Australian, British, and Indian.

Lessons I learned editing AI-narrated audiobooks:

- Google's available voices sound human, but they can't act. They can't emote. I attempt to compensate for this by using different voices for different characters.
- A possessive for a proper noun ending in "s" can be created by just having an apostrophe or an apostrophe and an "s." If you want the AI voice to pronounce it correctly, you need to have an apostrophe and an "s."
- You may need to change spellings in creative ways to have the AI voice pronounce some of your words correctly, especially unusual character names.
- Don't be surprised if by listening to the AI audiobook you discover that one typo, usually a missing or slightly misplaced word, that got through all your writing, revising, and editing efforts.

After your book is published, you can add "Content reviewers." Again, these are people who you want to receive your book at no charge. Perhaps they've agreed to review the book or they're people you want to check out your book set up. This is one of my favorite features on Google Play because it is super easy. All you have to do is add the person's email address.

The "Book info" tab will feature information transferred over from your EPUB. You should take a look at it to determine if there's anything you want to change for the audiobook. I would pay particular attention to the series page and the settings page. You will need to reupload a cover, but this time the document name should match the identifying number for your audiobook. You also need to set your prices. Google Play pays a 52% royalty rate on AI-narrated audiobooks.

Google Play: Marketing

Google Play has three built-in marketing opportunities that you can access through the "Promotions" tab on the left-hand side of the main page.

One option is to offer "Promotional pricing: For all customers." This means that you reduce the price for a set amount of time. Google Play may then promote this sale. I've done this with my first books in my series, and it has led to subsequent sales.

You can also set up promo codes that are limited to the people with whom you share the codes and series bundles. This means that if a reader buys all of the books in your series, they get a discount.

CHAPTER SIXTEEN

Apple

What Apple publishes: e-books and audiobooks
Where to start: https://itunesconnect.apple.com/

I publish my books on Apple through Smashwords/ Draft2Digital, an aggregator that I will discuss in Chapter Eighteen. I did try publishing directly on Apple a few years ago. I'm not keen on the platform, which felt fiddly to me, but if you want to publish directly on Apple here's how.

Reasons to publish directly on Apple:
- Slightly higher royalty rates
- Access to promotional programs
- A greater degree of control

Reasons to publish on Apple through an aggregator:
- One more platform to manage
- You need an Apple/Mac computer
- AI-narrated audiobooks need to go through an aggregator

Your first step is to create your iTunes Connect account

for Apple Books. If you already have an iTunes account, you can use that as your publisher account or set up a new one.

Note: Your Apple ID must have two-factor authentication enabled, and you must have a valid credit card on file.

Select "Books" from the list of possibilities, and select your publisher type, either "Organization" or "Individual." Input various tax and financial information. Agree to the terms and conditions.

Apple: E-books

To publish your e-book, open your previously formatted document with the Pages app on your Apple computer. Select "Publish to Apple Books" from the "File" menu if you are on a laptop or desktop. If you are on an iPad or iPhone, go to the three-dot menu in the right-hand corner and select "Publish to Apple Books" from the "Explore" menu.

Follow the prompts to sign into iTunes Connect. Choose the seller name under which you want to publish your book. Select "This is a new book." Click "Continue." Select a layout. Choose "Reflowable" for books that are mostly text. Choose "Fixed" for image-heavy or multi-column documents. Add your cover. Cover art must be in PNG or JPEG format, RGB color space, and at least 1,400 pixels on its shortest side. Complete the remaining book information fields and click "Continue." Preview your book, and then click "Upload." Then go to iTunes Connect to set a price for your book and choose where you want it to be available for purchase. Apple pays a 70% royalty rate.

Note: Your book can take up to 24 hours to appear in iTunes Connect. When it does, click on it and select "Rights and Pricing."

Don't forget to hit "Save."

Apple: Audiobooks

AI-narrated audiobooks launched on Apple at the beginning of 2023, but you need to publish through an aggregator such as Draft2Digital or Ingram to access this service.

Apple: Marketing

Apple allows the creation of up to 250 promo codes for each of your books published directly on this platform. These allow people, such as bloggers and reviewers, to download your book from Apple Books at no cost. Promo codes expire four weeks after they're requested.

CHAPTER SEVENTEEN

Barnes & Noble/Nook Press

What Barnes & Noble/Nook Press (B&N) publishes: e-books and paperbacks

Where to start: https://press.barnesandnoble.com/

My paperbacks are distributed to Nook.com through KDP's expanded distribution (Chapter Thirteen), and my e-books are distributed to this platform through Smashwords/Draft2Digital (Chapter Eighteen). I don't publish directly on B&N primarily because I don't see any advantage to doing so, although some authors have found success on this platform.

Reasons to publish directly on B&N:
- Slightly higher royalty rates
- Access to promotional programs
- A greater degree of control
- You can add contributors to your account.
- You control the pages and features these contributors, such as business partners or assistants, have access to including projects, sales reporting, promotions, etc.

Your contributors will sign in using their own email and password credentials with your unique link. This means you do not have to share your Barnes & Noble/Nook sign-in information with others who may need to work on your account.

- Access to vetted third-party sellers of publishing services such as cover design

Reasons to publish on B&N through an aggregator:

- One more platform to manage

If you want to publish directly on B&N here's how.

Your first step is to create an account on this platform. If you already have a B&N account to buy books, you can use it to create a publishing account. If you don't, you can create a publishing account from scratch. After the initial account creation, B&N will ask you to complete your vendor registration, which means filling out your publisher name, which is required but can be your pen name, and your website, which is optional. You will then need to answer questions about your citizenship, taxpayer status, and banking.

After everything is approved, which shouldn't take long, you are ready to publish on this platform.

To start publishing click on the "Projects" tab. Click on the blue "Create a new book" button. Select either "Print" or "E-book."

B&N: E-books

After you've selected "E-book" and clicked "Next," input your book's title. You have up to 120 characters. Click "Next." The next page gives you the option of setting up a pre-order. For e-books, your pre-order can be up to 12 months, and you will need a cover to get things started. Your cover should be a JPG or PNG file between 5KB and 2MB. The height and width should be at least 1,400 pixels. Your final version of the interior and cover of the e-book need to be uploaded at least 72 hours before publication. Any word processing program can be used to create an interior file, but Microsoft Word for Mac or PC or Mac Pages are recommended. Your file can be a DOC, DOCX, TXT, HTML, or EPUB.

The next screen asks for your title, subtitle, publisher name, publication date, edition number, edition description, and whether the book is part of a series. You can also input your default blurb (max of 2,000 characters) and an optional long blurb (max of 5,000 characters). The "Author" tab asks for up to five contributors to your work and biographies for all involved (max 2,500 characters each).

For the "Categories" tab, your first step is to identify your audience. This will dictate what categories are available for your book. For example, if you select "Mature," you shouldn't be able to select any kids or young adult categories. You will then choose your book's main language and indicate whether your book is fiction or nonfiction.

The next box allows you to select up to five categories most appropriate for your book. The first category you pick will be your primary category. You can change the order of categories after you select them. If you choose "General adult" for your audience and say that your book is fiction, you won't have access to any specifically lesbian categories, although there are loads of LGBT categories to choose from. The next box does give you a hundred characters for inputting keywords. You can input the word "lesbian" there.

And here's where things get weird. Keep in mind I don't usually publish directly on B&N. I go through Smashwords/Draft2Digital. I am going through the process now and writing it out for you in case you want to publish your books directly.

If you select "Mature" for your audience and say your book is fiction, you will have access to all the lesbian categories including:

Erotica>Lesbian Erotica

Erotica > Lesbian Erotica - General

LGBT Fiction - Teen Fiction > Lesbian fiction - Teen fiction - General

LGBT Fiction - Teen Fiction > Lesbian friendship and romance - Teen fiction

LGBT Fiction > Lesbian Fiction - Other

LGBT Fiction > Lesbian Identity - LGBT Fiction

LGBT Fiction > Lesbian Love, Romance & Relationships

Lesbian & Gay Life - Kids Fiction > Gay, lesbian and transgender people - Children's fiction

Romance > Other Romance Categories > Lesbian Romance - Other

Lesbian & Gay Life - Kids Fiction > Children of gay parents - Children's fiction

I don't publish children's books, so I wasn't initially going to look at the categories for children's book authors. Most of the kids' fiction categories above also appear if you are publishing for those under age 13.

Here's what's weird:

- Children's book categories shouldn't be available to those publishing books intended for a mature audience.
- Lesbian categories should be available for those publishing books for a general adult audience.

You can set your price on the next page. This platform pays 70% of cover price, which cannot be greater than the price on other sales channels or on your print edition if you have one. The subsequent "Rights and other information" page asks about digital right management (DRM), whether your book is in the public domain, and if you have your own ISBN. If you have any reviews in advance, you can enter up to five of them on the "Editorial reviews" tab.

The final page allows you to review everything you've input and to create coupon codes for your books.

B&N: Paperbacks

The process for a print book is similar, although a pre-order can be up to six months. Everything needs to be uploaded at least 10 days before the publication date. You also have the option of creating a print book for sale to the public or for personal use.

An interesting option is that you can create hardcovers with printed cases or dust jackets. These fancier versions can get pricey, but they could be an option if you want to create special editions. Another interesting aspect of uploading print books to this vendor is that for a cover, you can upload a full wrap (front cover, back cover, and spine) or just the back and front cover. Then B&N will add the spine and turn it into a full wrap for you.

B&N: Marketing

You can create coupon codes for your books that you can share with potential readers, much like several other platforms, but B&N has internal promotions that I've heard very good things about. You can email the company to request that a "Promotions" tab be added to your dashboard. This allows you to apply for their promotional opportunities. According to online discussions among self-published authors, getting the promotions tab can be random, and several authors report asking for it more than once and including flattery with the request emails that are successful.

CHAPTER EIGHTEEN

Publishing aggregators

An aggregator is a platform that takes your book and feeds it to multiple vendors. I've used Smashwords, the original publishing aggregator founded in 2008, to reach multiple book retailers since 2014 when I started self-publishing. There's a lot I love about this platform, which has its own marketplace and distributes to more than a dozen retailers. At the beginning of 2022, Draft2Digital, another aggregator founded in 2012, bought Smashwords. These two powerhouses in the self-publishing world are merging, which means things are about to change. Therefore, this chapter focuses on the generalities of publishing on several aggregators rather than the details of publishing on Smashwords, which will always have a special place in my heart. Self-published authors now have far more choices than when Smashwords was founded and when I started in this business.

Interesting, Draft2Digital also bought SelfPubBookcovers.com, a premade book cover marketplace in July 2023. It'll be interesting to see what they do with it and how it will be integrated into operations.

Note: Publishing aggregators frequently brag about the number of platforms they can get your book published on. The most important platforms are Apple, Nook, Kobo, and Scribd, which represent 99% of my sales through Smashwords, although I did have a random sale on Gardners, the United Kingdom's largest book wholesaler, in 2023. I'm not saying the other platforms aren't important or you won't have sales on them. I am saying that you want your chosen aggregator to play well with the platforms upon which you are likely to have the most sales.

Also note: Although you can publish directly on Apple, Nook, and Kobo, Scribd requires self-published authors to go through an aggregator.

And another note: IngramSpark is an aggregator. You can use it to create e-books, but it is primarily used by self-published authors for print book distribution. Therefore, this platform is explored in Chapter Twenty which focuses on getting your book into brick-and-mortar bookstores.

Now, let's get into who's who. I'm writing about Smashwords/Draft2Digital first. I then write about PublishDrive and Streetlib. I don't publish on those platforms, and there are other aggregators out there. Those are the ones I hear successful self-published authors talk about the most.

Smashwords/Draft2Digital

Where to start: http://www.smashwords.com/
and http://draft2digital.com/
For 2023, Smashwords is in the process of merging with Draft2Digital. According to statements made since the merger was announced in 2022, the plan is to keep Smashwords as a books marketplace while all self-publishing is to be handled by Draft2Digital. This makes sense and has received a lot of positive feedback in the self-

publishing community. The Smashwords marketplace is powerful. I've sold lots of books on it, and royalty rates are 80% or higher, which is about as good as it gets. I've used Smashwords coupons to give free or discounted books to my newsletter readers, and Smashwords has periodic platform wide sales that have served me well. Smashwords also has an erotica certification system and has long published some erotica that other platforms would not.

Smashwords (tagline: Your Book, Your Way) has a long history of being more DIY than Draft2Digital (tagline: Self-publishing With Support) which has more automation tools including automated back matter and universal book links. When I started self-publishing, Smashwords was an established player whereas Draft2Digital was a newbie. I, and I'm sure I'm not the only author who did this, would periodically agonize over whether I should shift over to Draft2Digital. I've always been a bit more DIY, so Smashwords worked well for me. I also always liked the marketplace, which is probably the main reason I stayed.

So, what does this mean for you, especially as a new self-published author?

Open an account on Draft2Digital. Smashwords no longer opens new author or publisher accounts, and all current self-publishing accounts are expected to transition to Draft2Digital by the end of 2023.

What you need to know about publishing on Draft2Digital:

- It costs nothing upfront to upload your books and publish on this platform.
- Draft2Digital takes 10% of your royalties. An example of what that means: If you publish on Apple through Draft2Digital, you will end up with approximately 60% of the cover price because Apple pays 70% and Draft2Digital takes a 10% cut.
- Accepted formats include DOC, DOCX, and EPUB, although they can work with anything Microsoft Word can read.

- You can create print books and e-books.
- You can access Apple's AI-narrated audiobook program, which is in beta.
- You can create coupons valid for your books on the Smashwords sales platform.
- They offer free ISBNs.
- They'll do a lot of formatting for you, including creating automated end matter.
- They distribute to:
  - Amazon
  - Apple Books
  - Barnes & Noble
  - Kobo (including Kobo Plus)
  - Smashwords Store
  - Tolino
  - OverDrive
  - Bibliotheca
  - Scribd
  - Baker & Taylor
  - Hoopla
  - Vivlio
  - BorrowBox
  - Odilo
- You get to choose which vendors to include or exclude.
- Other cool features include universal book links and preorder setup with most vendors.
- Pays monthly as long as the following thresholds are met.
  - Paypal ($0 USD minimum)
  - Direct deposit ($0 USD minimum)
  - International Direct Deposit ($10 USD minimum)
  - Payoneer ($20 USD minimum)
  - Check ($100 USD minimum)

- Draft2Digital emails you each time a book goes live on a platform. They also keep you updated on the status of your book at the other retailers.
- You can use their free book templates.
- You can set up a free author page that can substitute for a full website.
- For your e-book cover, they need a JPEG. The 1,600 x 2,400 pixels size is preferred, but they will work with any "tall rectangle." Book covers must include the book's title and the author's name.
- For a print book cover, Draft2Digital will automatically generate a wraparound cover based on your e-book art (front cover art), and they provide some basic customization options like spine text and back cover text editing.
- EPUBs created by Draft2Digital can be downloaded and sold on other vendors.

PublishDrive

Where to start: https://publishdrive.com
What you need to know about publishing on PublishDrive:
- After a free trial, it costs $9.99 for the basic plan, which includes publishing two books, but you keep 100% of your royalties. The price goes up the more books you want to publish.
- Accepted formats include DOCX and EPUB.
- Publishes print, e-books, and audiobooks.
- You have to do your own formatting.
- Distributes print on demand paperbacks to:
  - Amazon
  - Ingram
  - China Print
- Distributes e-books to:
  - Amazon

- o Apple Books
- o Google Play Books
- o Kobo
- o Barnes and Noble
- o Scribd
- o Overdrive.com
- o Dangdang
- o CNPeReading
- o Playster
- o Odilo.es
- o Bookmate.com
- o Gardners.com
- o Mackin.com
- o Perlego
- o Ciando.com
- o 24symbols.com
- o Bibliotheca
- o E-sentral.com
- o Ekonyv.hu
- o Ultimediaplaza.com
- o Bookshout!
- o Tolino
- o E-letoltes
- o Tookbook.com
- o Elefant.ro
- ▪ Distributes audiobooks to:
  - o Apple Audiobooks
  - o Audible
  - o Google Play Audio
  - o Kobo Audio
  - o Overdrive Audio
  - o Bookmate Audio
  - o CNPeReading Audio
  - o Findaway
  - o Gardners Audio
  - o Voxa Audio

- o Lazyjoy Audio
- o Storytel Audio
- o Empik Group Audio
- You can access Amazon Advertising through this platform, and the subscription comes with some ad credits.
- You can set up price promotions by store.
- You can offer free review copies.
- You have to provide your own ISBNs.
- You have to earn $5 minimum in royalties to get paid.
- A lot of people like the interface and the reporting dashboard.

StreetLib

Where to start: https://www.streetlib.com
What you need to know about publishing on StreetLib:
- Possibly the widest distribution network of any aggregator.
- Distributes to 50+ platforms including the most important ones.
- Distributes e-books, paperbacks, and audiobooks.
- No upfront costs for e-books and audiobooks. Takes a percentage of royalties, 10% for e-books and 20% for audiobooks.
- Costs 49 Euro to distribute print books, plus a 10% of cover price activation cost for each title.
- Free ISBNs.
- StreetLib Write is a software that will lay out your book. It has a free tier, but the ones that cost money are priced at 4.99 Euros and 8.99 Euros.
- You can organize promotional and discount campaigns by platform.
- Automated conversion from Word to EPUB.
- You can customize prices for each store.

- Has a mobile app.

CHAPTER NINETEEN

Audiobook publishers

Audiobooks are a fast-growing segment of the literary world. Some of the platforms and aggregators that publish and distribute e-books and print books also publish and distribute audiobooks. I cover those details in the chapters for those platforms. This chapter is focused on dedicated audiobook publishers including ACX, which is owned by Amazon and publishes to Amazon, Audible, and iTunes, and Author's Republic and Findaway Voices, both of which are aggregators distributing to numerous platforms.

Note: Audiobooks are books. This is not open for discussion.

Also note: There are many other companies that publish and distribute audiobooks. I also know some authors publish their audiobooks on YouTube, earning money from advertising. You have a lot of options in this space. The ones I'm presenting here are the ones that I'm most familiar with and that I hear other self-published authors say good things about the most often.

ACX (Audiobook Creation Exchange)

Where to start: https://www.acx.com/
I haven't published on ACX. but it's the big player in this space. It distributes to Amazon, Audible, and iTunes and royalty rates vary from 20% to 40%, depending on whether you are willing to make your audiobook exclusive to this platform. For example, you can pay your producer (also known as your narrator) a flat fee and earn 40% of each sale if you are exclusive. Non-exclusivity earns you 25%.

Note: Narrators/producers generally cost $50-$400 per finished recorded hour.

The same royalty rates apply if you narrate the book yourself or work with a narrator/producer unaffiliated with the ACX platform. There's also a royalty share option. This requires exclusivity but no out of pocket costs. You earn 20% of your sales while your narrator/producer who you find on the ACX platform receives the other 20%. The royalty share plus option requires a direct payment to the narrator and a share of royalties. A growing number of narrators will only accept this arrangement.

You will receive monthly sales statements, but you have to earn at least $50 before ACX will make a payment to you. In addition to your royalties, you can earn a $75 "bounty" if the first audiobook someone listens to is your book. This is your reward for turning someone into an audiobook customer.

Note: ACX sets your book's price. These are the general guidelines for the possible prices.
- under 1 hour: under $7
- 1 - 3 hours: $7 - $10
- 3 - 5 hours: $10 - $20
- 5 - 10 hours: $15 - $25
- 10 - 20 hours: $20 - $30
- over 20 hours: $25 - $35

Another note: The distribution deal for these

arrangements is seven years.

Your first step is to visit ACX and login using your Amazon account. The first time you login, you will be asked for some basic information including your name and address. On the next screen you can set up your payment and tax information as well as start producing your audiobook.

In the top right-hand corner, you should see "Add your title." Your book must be published on Amazon to be able to use ACX for audiobook production. I didn't have much luck searching by my name, but my books did pop up when I typed in the ASIN, the unique number that Amazon assigns e-books. When you find your book, click the purple button that says, "This is my book."

Keep in mind: Don't claim any books that aren't yours, and only try to create an audiobook out of your book if you have the right to do so. If you self-published your book, you'll have the rights. If you published through a publishing company, you'll need to read your contract.

The next pop up will ask you if you have audio files ready to upload or if you are looking to hire a producer/narrator.

Any audio files you upload must be of good quality, include opening and closing credits, have a retail sample between one and five minutes long, and be recorded by a human being. No AI voices are allowed.

If you need to create audio files, the next step is to create a title profile which will include a description of your book, copyright information, and the type of narrator needed. There isn't a specific lesbian category, but there is an LGBTQ+ category. Your narrator can be male, female, or gender neutral. A range of accents, ages, and styles are available. You also need a one- or two-page excerpt from your book. This will act as your audition script. A space for "Additional comments" is an opportunity to provide directions and advice to producers who audition. This space is also a chance for you to provide marketing plans, selling points, bestseller status, awards, reviews, and social media reach. This is especially critical if you are hiring a narrator on a royalty share basis. They need to know the likelihood of your book selling.

After your request is out there, you can review available narrators and invite them to audition. You may have some come to you and ask for an opportunity to audition. If your book is fiction, make sure the narrator can voice your different characters.

You can review auditions and make an offer. Once a narrator/producer accepts an offer, you are ready to move forward. The narrator will initially record and upload a 15-minute checkpoint or sample for you to approve and/or provide feedback. Once the sample is approved, the narrator will proceed to record your full book.

When your audiobook is ready, you need to listen to it. You can ask for up to two rounds of corrections. After you have approved your audiobook, pay your narrator/producer unless you're on a royalty share deal.

You also need a cover. It must be square and a JPG, PNG, or TIF file format only. Your cover should be no smaller than 2,400 x 2,400 pixels, 72 dpi resolution. Other requirements include that it be 24-bit (True Color) minimum and RGB color (not CYMK). The file name should be a condensed version of your book title with alphanumeric characters only. Rectangular art is not accepted, nor are rectangular images with borders added to fill out the space. Your cover must include your title, and there can't be any references to competing marketplaces, soliciting for 3rd party websites, personal information, or URLs to external sites/contacts. There also shouldn't be references to run time or pricing.

It is now time to distribute. If you are exclusive, this part of the process is done. If you are non-exclusive, you can take your audio files and distribute them through additional channels.

After your audiobook is out there, the main

opportunities to promote on ACX are promotional codes. These can be distributed to reviewers who can redeem the code for a free copy of your audiobook. Once your first 10 codes have been redeemed and your catalog of titles has reached 100 qualified sales, you may request an additional 25 codes per marketplace.

Some authors have reported that, without notification, their book sometimes gets designated an "Audible book of the day," which causes sales to spike. This is strictly at Audible's whim. You can't request it, and they don't warn you that it's coming. I hope this happens to you, and that your book is chosen.

Note: ACX has by far the biggest reach, but authors frequently complain that the sales reporting dashboard is murky. And no one likes the seven-year contract, which feels like such a long time.

Findaway Voices

Where to start: https://findawayvoices.com/
Findaway Voices, which is owned by Spotify, is an aggregator that has a partnership with Smashwords/ Draft2Digital. If your books are published on Smashwords/ Draft2Digital, you can access Findaway through a "create audiobooks" button on Smashwords/Draft2Digital's dashboard. The possibility to create an audiobook also appears just after you publish your e-book on that platform. This is a nice option because all your book's metadata transfers over.

You do not have to be published on Smashwords/ Draft2Digital to create and publish audiobooks through Findaway.

Note: You can publish to Audible through Findaway, but many self-published authors publish directly through ACX and then use Findaway or another aggregator for all other vendors.

Also note: You want to balance all decisions on the time and expense required. For example, you may (or may not) do better financially by publishing on ACX and Findaway, but is it worth your time? And never forget your goals. They're more important than anyone else's.

Your first step is to create an account on Findaway Voices. You will then be able to answer a short questionnaire about your audiobook's emotional tone, accents, dialects, voice style, and heat level among other factors. This information will be used by Findaway to recommend six to ten professional voice actors for your consideration. You can also peruse their database. Recommendations will include audio samples and hourly rates for each narrator. You can request audition samples where narrators create sample readings of your book. You also have the option of creating an author page to help narrators get to know you.

Production begins after you select your narrator and sign off on the production contract. You will pay production fees directly to Findaway Voices. Fees are based on the number of hours and minutes of the finished production. Each hour of recorded content is comprised of roughly 9,000 words. Narrators typically charge between $150 and $400 per finished hour.

Findaway does have its "Voices Share" program, which is similar to ACX's Royalty Share Plus. Authors pay half the upfront cost of making an audiobook and commit to giving 20% of their royalties to their narrator for the next ten years. If you want to cut that time short, there are buyout options.

When production completes, you'll control all rights to the audiobook and can set your price. You have the option to distribute your audiobook to more than 40 outlets including:

- Apple iTunes
- Audible
- Scribd

- OverDrive
- Google Play
- Kobo/Walmart
- Beek
- Nook
- eStories
- Audiobooks.com
- TuneIn
- 24Symbols
- Anyplay

Note: Some of these vendors such as Overdrive mean your audiobook will be distributed to libraries. Before I discovered bookstores, I discovered the local library. I support anything that makes my e-books, paperbacks, hardbacks, and audiobooks more accessible to libraries.

Things to know about Findaway:

- You can create an audiobook before your e-book/paperback is published, except for Audible.
- Human narrators only; no AI narration.
- The various platforms pay 20% to 50% royalty rates. Findaway takes 20% of that, except for Spotify. Spotify pays 50%, and Findaway does not take a cut of that.
- You can create free Spotify promotional cards for your audiobook.

Your cover must be a PNG, TIF, or JPG file, minimum 72 DPI resolution, 24-bit color, and 2,400 x 2,400 pixels. Square cover art is required without the use of borders or letterboxing. Cover needs to include the book's title, author(s), and series info and must match the metadata exactly.

To promote your audiobook, Findaway Voices supplies you with 100 codes that people can redeem to get the book for free on Spotify. Findaway is also linked with Chirp, Bookbub's audiobook promotion service. You control your price on Findaway Voices and have the ability to regularly set promotional pricing. They also send out periodic calls for authors to discount their audiobooks. These discounts are then pitched to major audiobook sellers.

Author's Republic.

Where to start: https://www.authorsrepublic.com/
Author's Republic is another popular audiobook aggregator. It has access to over fifty retail channels, library platforms, and music streaming services and takes 30% of any royalties earned. Unlike Findaway or ACX, this platform can't do pre-orders, but it has a good-looking interface.

Note: I am just starting to publish audiobooks, and I've found the whole process overwhelming. I will say that after writing this chapter I will most likely work with an aggregator such as Findaway Voices or Author's Republic.

CHAPTER TWENTY

Brick-and-mortar bookstores

I dithered about whether to include a chapter on this topic. Independent bookstores are the best places on Earth and should be supported. Many authors dream of seeing their books on the shelf of a bookstore. However, most books are bought from online vendors. This is especially true for those that are self-published. Large bookstore chains are falling like dominos. The number of independent bookstores is shrinking.

But I've never been one to stand in the way of anyone's dreams.

Note: Whatever happens and whatever your interactions with those who run bookstores when trying to convince them to stock your books, don't hold a grudge and don't talk smack about anyone. Brick-and-mortar bookstores, especially independent ones, are small businesses, and they were struggling before the COVID-19 pandemic. After the pandemic shutdowns, many small businesses are one bad sales day away from bankruptcy.

We're lucky to have them. It may not make business sense for them to stock your book. Some of them are so overwhelmed by pitches from self-published authors that they now charge upwards of $50 to review self-published books for possible sale in their store. I suspect this is more of a deterrent than a true moneymaker, but it does speak to a dire situation. Independent bookstores do not have time to deal with you. Don't take any of this personally. Always support independent bookstores.

Having said all that, here's how you might get your book on the shelves of a brick-and-mortar bookstore.

You could visit one, sneak your book onto the shelf, enjoy looking at it for a minute, take a photo, take your book off the shelf, and then buy something else from them.

If that's not enough and you want your book to actually be on sale at a brick-and-mortar bookstore, there are a few things you can do. You can approach a few local bookstores after checking their websites to find out their policies about self-published books if they have them. For example, I live in a neighborhood with several small bookstores. One consistently gives me the brush. One will accept self-published books on a consignment basis. One has a GoFundMe that is always accepting donations, which makes me concerned about their financial viability.

You can get your books into local bookstores, but it may take some shoe leather. With everything in self-publishing, it's important to ask if it's worth your time.

Another option is to publish with IngramSpark. I currently publish my paperbacks through KDP and use their "Expanded distribution" option. This gets my paperbacks into Bookshop.org, Waterstones (online), Bol.com, and several other online bookstores. It will not, however, get me into traditional brick-and-mortar bookstores.

For that, you need the much wider distribution network of IngramSpark. You need to discount your book for bookstores, and you have to allow returns, which is standard for brick-and-mortar bookstores. Many self-published authors distribute their paperbacks and hardbacks to Amazon through KDP. They **don't** select expanded distribution and use Ingram to distribute paper books to everyone else. Everyone else includes a global distribution network of 40,000 retailers, bookstores, online stores, libraries, and universities.

Note: You can also use IngramSpark to print books that you sell yourself with or without using them for global distribution.

Also note: Ingram can print paperbacks, case laminate hardbacks, and way cool, hardcover books with dust jackets.

And another thing: Even if a bookstore doesn't carry your book on its bookshelves, you can encourage your readers to order your book through their local bookstore. This means that you get a sale, and the bookstore gets a cut. Everyone wins.

IngramSpark

Where to start: https://www.ingramspark.com/
Your first step is to create an account on IngramSpark, which just requires your name, an email address, and acknowledgement that you are not a robot. You also need to agree to the privacy policy. Receiving their promotional emails is optional. After you have verified your email address, you have 30 days to look around and complete your full account set up. If you decide not to move forward after 30 days, your data will be deleted.

To complete your registration, you will most likely select a personal account since you are an author publishing your own work. Input your legal name (not your pen name), address, and phone number. You will need to verify your phone number and accept the agreement, which may look dull but includes a lot of important information like the fact that you can change the price of your book no more than once every seven days and other interesting tidbits.

The additional optional opportunities include agreements to distribute digital titles to Amazon, which you can't participate in if you've published any books with KDP in the past year, and Apple. There's also an optional agreement to distribute print titles to Target.com.

Note: Ingram does publish e-books, but it's not recommended to publish your e-books through them. They are a must if you want to get your paperbacks or hardbacks into brick-and-mortar bookstores. For these reasons, this chapter will only be going through publishing print books on Ingram, not e-books.

I accepted the optional agreement to distribute print titles to Target.com but not the ones to distribute e-books to Amazon or Apple. I'm already on Amazon direct through KDP, and I access Apple through Smashwords/ Draft2Digital.

Your next steps include adding your bank account information so you can be paid and your credit card information, so you can pay them for services.

Then you are ready to publish. Click the "Print book only" button and let's get going. You will then be asked whether you have files ready to go or need to see the available options for creating files such as Ingram's own book building tool. You also have the option to enter information about your book but submit the files later.

If you click the button saying your files are ready, you will be asked to confirm that you have a print-ready pdf of your cover and interior and that both these files meet their file creation requirements. You also have the option to ask Ingram to "Print, Distribute, and Sell" your book through its global distribution network or just print it for you to distribute and sell yourself.

Clicking the box asking to see available options for creating print ready files gives you the option of using

Ingram's book building tool or hiring an expert.

Note: There's nothing wrong with hiring someone, but always remember that as a self-published author, you're in charge.

Clicking the box saying you will enter your information and upload your files later will take you directly to the metadata screen. There you can enter your title, language, and ISBN. You can publish using your own ISBN or one provided by Ingram. If you use the one provided by Ingram, the publisher will be listed as "Indy Pub," and the book must participate in Ingram's wholesale distribution program. You then need to confirm your publishing rights. Click on the "Show more fields to improve optimization" to input your subtitle, series, and edition information, which are all optional.

The next row asks about authors and contributors. At least one author name is required, and the drop-down menu gives you the option of adding your (or your pen name's) location, biography, prior work, and affiliations as well as information about other contributors.

You can then input your imprint (or publisher name) and categories. These are referred to as subjects, and you can choose three. The most likely for a lesbian novel are:
- fiction/erotica/LGBTQ+/lesbian
- fiction/romance/LGBTQ+/lesbian
- fiction/LGBTQ+/lesbian

Your audience for most lesbian novels, unless they are YA, will be "trade/general adult." The next box asks for your title description (blurb; maximum 4,000 bytes) and keywords. The drop-down menu gives you the option of adding a short description (250 bytes).

Yes, Ingram measures in bytes, not characters, although it appears that one byte is approximately one character.

Hit "Continue" to move on to the "print info" page or "save and exit" to take a break. On this page, you choose your trim size, and select your pricing and return policies for the U.S., the United Kingdom, European Union, Canada,

Australia, and Global Connect. You choose a wholesaler discount of between 40% and 55%, although 55% is recommended, and your return policies. You can choose to not accept returns, which means bookstores will not have the option to return the books they buy from IngramSpark; return and destroy, which means they can get a refund for returned books that are then destroyed; or return and ship to you. Shipping and handling fees average about $3.00 per book. You will also be charged the wholesale price of the book that is returned.

A note about returns: This is an area where many authors have struggled and sometimes get unpleasant surprises. It's been my main reason for not publishing on IngramSpark. Most authors say they've only received a handful of returns, which is a minimal cost and worth it because of all the sales they make as a result of Ingram's reach. However, sometimes returns result in thousands of dollars in chargebacks that can be quite a shock. I do intend to use Ingram going forward, and I will allow returns. I hope I don't regret it.

Things to know about publishing on IngramSpark:
- Setting up your title is free, but Ingram takes 1% of the local list price at the time of sale.
- Revisions within the first 60 days of production are free. They cost $25 each after 60 days.
- If you create your own PDF in Microsoft Word, do not use the "Shortcut" button/icon in the toolbar. Use the print menu and "Print" to PDF.
- Ensure all fonts are embedded into the PDF file.
- It's recommended to use their cover template generator that can be accessed through the "My tools" tab. Input your book's information and a cover template will be emailed to you along with instructions for cover creation.
- Your file name should be your ISBN followed by the book title.

- Each format (paperback, hard cover, etc.) must have its own ISBN, and the correct ISBN needs to be included on the title page.
- Books fewer than 48 pages can't have any text on the spine.
- It's advised to not use Ingram to distribute your paperback to Amazon. Rather, distribution of paperbacks to Amazon should be handled by KDP.

PART III: THE ADVENTURE CONTINUES

CHAPTER TWENTY-ONE

Now what?

So, maybe you've written that book you've had in your head for years. Maybe you published it. Maybe you had a few sales. Maybe people you didn't even know bought your book. Maybe you had a lot of sales.

Or not. That's okay too.

About those goals

Now is a great time to revisit those goals of yours that I've mentioned several times in this book. Do they still fit you? Do you need to tweak them? Do you need completely new goals? Have there been any unintended consequences—both good and bad—of your writing and publishing efforts? How have they impacted your goals? How have they impacted you?

I mention goals because I frequently see authors moaning, "When am I going to make it?" I also see some authors satisfied with what they've achieved, but who feel pressured to do more than they really want to.

If you don't know what success means for you (your goals), you'll end up frustrated. If you don't know where you're going, you'll never get there. Spend some time identifying what's important to you. It may also be time to identify what motivates you. I love selling lesbian fiction in countries where I am illegal. I love when a book I wrote years ago has a random sale. I adore fan letters. You most likely have your own motivations.

A person commented on my most recent TikTok video that one of my books was her go-to that she liked to read over and over again. Swoon. Be still my heart.

Someone once told me that tension is who you think you should be. Relaxation is who you are. I think about that a lot.

Building a support network

As you consider your goals, now is also a great time to look at your support network (in-person and online; online friends count). Maybe several people in your life were less than supportive? Maybe some of your friends are great to see a movie with, but real downers when it came to your publishing efforts. You can still go to the movies with those people, but you're going to have to meet new friends who better understand your writing and publishing journey.

My father once told me, "The heart of another is a dark forest."

He, of course, stole that from Willa Cather, but the point is that no one can ever truly and fully understand another person. I've been with my wife for more than 15 years, and I don't even understand why she loads the dishwasher the way she does.

However, you need people in your life who have at least some understanding of what you are trying to do even if sometimes it doesn't feel like 100%. Don't be so picky that you never connect with anyone. As much as I'd love to connect with another lesbian writing and self-publishing lesbian fiction who lives on my block (or even my city), it's okay if they don't fulfill all of my criteria. Or fill the dishwasher the same as I do. It's okay to have some things in common and not others. I've learned a lot about writing and publishing from people who didn't write in my genre and weren't lesbians. Connect where you can. Don't expect anyone to be your everything.

So, how do you meet people who are self-publishing, especially those who are self-publishing lesbian fiction?

A lot of discussion about self-publishing happens on Facebook in groups such as 20Booksto50k®, Wide For the Win (still on Facebook, but has moved a lot of discussion to Circle), the Lesfic Marketing Alliance, or the I Heart SapphFic Author Forum, and you can make connections there. In person opportunities include various writing conferences such as 20Booksto50k® (about to be renamed) which happens in Las Vegas every November or the Golden Crown Literary Society (lesbian writers) annual conference which is in a different city every year. You may also be able to find local writers groups that serve your needs.

Note: The choice, as always, is yours but I generally avoid writers' conferences or events focused primarily on finding an agent or that present self-publishing as a get rich quick scheme. I'm not interested in an agent, and self-publishing is not a get rich quick scheme.

Relaunching your books

If you've published your book (or maybe two), it's fine to rest on your laurels and stop there.

Or maybe you're ready for more.

If some time has passed since you wrote and published your baby, I mean your book, is it time for a relaunch? Self-publishing means you can constantly learn and improve your skills. Are you now better at picking categories and devising keywords? Is it time to revisit your metadata and make it better? What about a new cover? Maybe you caught a typo, and you want to fix it? Maybe you're a better writer, and you want to rewrite the whole thing? It's your book. You can do whatever you want with it. I recommend Chris Fox's *Relaunch Your Novel* as a guide for this.

Expanding your publishing efforts

As part of the relaunch process, it's worth asking whether you can expand to other formats and other markets. What about turning your e-book into an audiobook? Would a hardcover serve your market? If you didn't publish on all the platforms I've already discussed, is it time to consider doing so? A growing number of established self-published authors are selling their books directly from their websites. Would this be a good option for you?

Note: Never feel like you have to do everything. Your time is your most precious resource. You can make more money. You can't make more time.

Also note: In-person direct selling is discussed in Chapter Ten. The next section discusses selling your books from your website.

Direct selling

Some authors are setting up TikTok shops. Important caveat: If you don't ship out your book in three days, TikTok will cancel the order.

Many more are setting up to be able to sell from their own website. Your first step is to set up your website, and your next step is to set up your online store. The most popular option is Shopify which has a monthly charge, although your first month is free. Other choices are WooCommerce, which is free but requires Wordpress, although it has nice integrations with Bookvault, which is used to print books on demand, or Gumroad, which is primarily used to sell digital creative assets such as Photoshop brushes. Other popular choices include Payhip. Many authors use Bookfunnel to deliver e-books and audiobooks. Lulu is also an interesting option, and you can create your own store on that platform. What I find most interesting about Lulu is the opportunity to create spiral bound books which I could see doing if I create a workbook to accompany this book.

With this kind of direct selling, you really are 100% in charge of and responsible for marketing with minimal if any organic reach from a platform, but a growing number of authors are finding success with this strategy.

CHAPTER TWENTY-TWO

Final words

So, we're here, nearly the last chapter. This has been an interesting journey for me, and I hope it's been good for you. I've poured everything I've learned over the past decade about successfully self-publishing lesbian fiction into this book.

Self-publishing is such a wonderful opportunity for lesbian fiction authors. Before self-publishing became so accessible, I hit a lot of barriers getting my stories out into the world. The publishing industry wasn't that interested in lesbian fiction, and I had no way of reaching the readers I knew were out there, the people who I knew wanted and needed my stories, lesbian stories, queer stories, our stories. Self-publishing eliminates those barriers. No one is between me and the readers I know are out there who want to buy and read my books. No one has to be between you and the readers who want your stories, too.

There are so many options. It's important to choose the option that best fits your needs as a creative professional. I hope I gave you some good guidance that moved you toward your goals, but even more importantly, your dreams, whatever they are.

Note: Don't check your sales figures too often. That can drive you crazy. I recommend no more than once a day, although I never follow that advice, so you do you.

And a nearly final word:

Self-publishing: not a get rich quick scheme, but it sure is fun.

It's important to manage your expectations as a self-published author. Success in any endeavor is never guaranteed, and it is important to be realistic about your goals and expectations. I hope you're successful beyond your wildest dreams and mine because that is possible. Remember that writing and self-publishing is a long-term investment, and success often comes from persistence and dedication.

More than anything I hope you keep writing and that it always gives you joy. I hope you keep sharing your stories with the world, and I look forward to reading your book(s).

CHAPTER TWENTY-THREE

10 reasons self-published authors should be terribly proud of themselves

1. You wrote a book.
2. You wrote a book that you are willing to let other people read.
3. You wrote a book that you are willing to let strangers read.
4. You wrote a book that you consider good enough for people to pay for the privilege of reading.
5. You wrote a book and identified the team of people (editors, proofreaders, cover designers, book designers, beta-readers, general supporters) that you needed to get it out into the world.
6. You didn't wait for someone else to tell you that you were good enough to publish.
7. You bring stories to the world that traditional publishing may not recognize as marketable or saleable. You publish anyway. You know your audience, and you

deliver to them what they have been waiting on for so long.

8. You have figured out how to format a manuscript so that it looks good on Amazon, Smashwords, and other e-book vendors.

9. You have figured out your own way to get the word out about your work.

10. You have figured out your own way to have fun and profit, and that is what you should be proud of most of all.

CHAPTER TWENTY-FOUR

Bad advice self-published authors have been given about writing and self-publishing

For some reason, people have no hesitation giving writers advice. When it's from people who have never self-published, let alone written a book, it can be particularly bad. Here's some of the worst advice authors of queer fiction have received and some snappy responses.

Note: This is bad advice that I and other authors have received, not advice from us. If anyone in your life gives you this advice, don't listen.

Bad advice writers have been given about writing

> *"Get kidnapped and write a book about it.*
> *That book will really sell."—advice I*
> *received from a high school classmate.*

> *"Don't use adverbs. Eliminate all words that*
> *end in 'ly' because they're unnecessary or*
> *redundant," bad advice received by Anne*
> *Hagan.*

*"Delete all the adjectives and adverbs from
your book. All of them. Get rid. Your book
will read better, and be more appealing, as a
direct result," bad advice given to KJ Charles.*

Some people really have a thing against adjectives and especially adverbs. That's too bad. Adverbs can be terribly useful.

See what I did there.

I wouldn't go overboard with them. You want your nouns and verbs to be strong and well-chosen, but the occasional adjective or adverb can be a good thing.

Other bad advice with regard to writing focuses on the subject and what you should and should not write.

*"Write what you know (meaning what
happened in your life)." is advice Liam
Livings has been given, and it's a common
one.*

*"'ONLY write what you know.' My
English teacher told me that. Imagine how
few crime novels there'd be if authors stuck to
that. How little sci-fi? Research is a
thing."—Lee Winter*

*"Write only what you know."—Wendy
Rathbone*

This is such common advice, and it's terrible, primarily because it is widely misinterpreted as meaning that you should write your life story. If you want to write a memoir or autobiography, great. If you want to write fiction, take your life story and set it on a space station or add vampires. Maybe do both.

"Stay in your lane–write in one genre."—Rebecca Cohen. Their response. "For me it is the way madness lies— it stifles creativity and the words will dry up. My voice is my brand not my lane and that carries over all the sub-genres I write in.”

One of the many wonderful things about self-publishing is being able to write what you want, and that may mean a bit of genre hopping.

> *“If you write fast, you can't write well.”—*
> *Wendy Rathbone*

The other wonderful thing is that you can publish as many or as few books as you want. You can write as fast or as slow as you want, and, yes, you can write well.

Others received bad advice, from a beta reader who just had it all wrong.

> *“After complaining that my epic fantasy*
> *novel didn’t have enough men in it (she called*
> *the primarily female cast ‘unfair’), a beta*
> *reader asked me why a particular character*
> *wasn’t a man because she had many*
> *‘mannish’ qualities. I asked her to clarify.*
> *The examples she gave boiled down to the*
> *character being confident, patient, and often*
> *wearing armor.”—SD Simper.*

Some writers get told a definition of success or even what defines someone as a writer.

> *“If you’re not a six-figure author, you have*
> *failed.” is something Ripley Hayes has been*
> *told.*

What I say: If you write, if you publish, you are outrageously successful. Refer to Chapter Twenty-three for more reasons to always feel successful and proud whether you earn six figures or one or nothing. Six figures would be nice, but no published writer is a failure. Yes, self-publishing counts as being published. (The debate over whether self-publishing is really publishing periodically flares on social media. They can kiss my tuchus.) It's important to stay focused on your goals. I know that we live in a capitalist society which means money is critical for survival, but I hope you have the luxury of having some non-monetary goals.

> *"If you don't write full time then you're not a proper writer." is bad advice Rebecca Cohen has been given.*

What I say: Full-time, part-time, occasional time, you're a proper writer.

> *"Follow (insert latest self-styled author guru) they're amazing'. And then we find out that the author guru has fabricated their work experience, they're running some kind of scam to funnel authors to their friend's editing/marketing/cover art business, or they do workshops on the writing process yet don't even write the books they sell. I guess what I'm saying is beware of false idols."—Isobel Starling*

You should listen to Isobel.

> *"If you follow all the received wisdom about self-publishing, you *will* make lots of money," is bad advice Liam Livings has received.*

This one made me laugh out loud. Sales are never guaranteed. You can do everything right, and the book won't move. You can do everything wrong, and you can't keep up with your sales. Whatever happens, I hope you enjoy the process.

> *"You have to spend money to make*
> *money."—bad advice given to Lissa Kasey*

So much about self-publishing is either no cost or low cost. Self-publishing is not expensive.

> *"Just write what is hot/selling and then later*
> *write the things you actually enjoy," is bad*
> *advice Stephanie Rose has been given.*

Here's the thing about writing what's "hot" at the moment. If you chase trends, you will always be behind. If you write what you enjoy, your joy will be readily apparent and very attractive to readers. And who knows, your genre may get really popular, and you'll be ready.

> *"If you write to market you're selling out," is*
> *bad advice Wendy Rathbone has received.*

I always say that if you're going to sell out, you should get a good price, but this issue is irrelevant. Writing what someone wants to read—that's a beautiful thing.

And the worst advice that many self-published authors have received is:

> *"Don't self publish."—JC Rycroft*

I'm so glad JC and my fellow authors in this chapter did not follow that bad advice. Well, that was fun. Thank you to my fellow authors for sharing the bad advice they have received. You should check out their books. They're good.

APPENDIX

Resources

20booksto50k®: Facebook group with more than 70,000 members. Focused on the business of self-publishing but also talks about craft. Hosts an annual conference in Las Vegas that is about to be renamed. https://www.facebook.com/groups/20Booksto50k/

Alliance of Independent Authors: Global membership association for self-published authors. Carries out a lot of advocacy on our behalf. Also, excellent educational resources. https://www.allianceindependentauthors.org/

BookBub: A behemoth in the book promotions world. They have numerous paid promotional opportunities and a few free ones. https://www.bookbub.com/launch

Bryan Cohen Has a very popular (and free) five-day ad challenge that he runs several times a year. Also runs several paid courses. https://bryancohen.com/

Golden Crown Literary Society: Nonprofit organization supporting an international community of readers, writers, publishers, editors, audiobook narrators, and fans devoted to increasing the diversity, accessibility, quality, and visibility of Sapphic and women-loving-women literature. Resources include an awards program, an annual conference, a writing school, and periodic educational opportunities. https://www.goldencrownliterarysociety.org/

Grammarly: Online grammar checker, style editor, proofreader, and writing coach. https://www.grammarly.com/

I Heart SapphFic: A hub for Sapphic readers and writers. https://iheartsapphfic.com/

I Heart SapphFic: Author Forum Facebook group of authors of lesbian, Sapphic, and woman-loving-woman fiction organized by the website of the same name. Organizes virtual writing sprints that can be fun. https://www.facebook.com/groups/ihlauthorforum/

Independent Book Publishers Association: Has really good criteria for evaluating hybrid publishers. https://www.ibpa-online.org/

IReadIndies International, Inc: Non-profit serving indie authors of Sapphic literature.
 https://www.ireadindies.com/

Lesfic ARC Club Facebook group of lesfic, Sapphic, and WLW authors offering free books to readers in exchange for honest reviews. I run this group. https://www.facebook.com/groups/1383788328317216/

Lesfic Marketing Alliance: Facebook group of authors of lesbian, Sapphic, and woman-loving-woman fiction. I'm a co-administrator. https://www.facebook.com/groups/233876183742675

MyQueerSapphFic: Email newsletter that offers paid promotional opportunities and is probably the best opportunity for queer, lesbian, and Sapphic books. https://www.myqueersapphfic.com/

ProWritingAid: An online grammar checker, style editor, proofreader, and writing coach that periodically holds some free nifty virtual conferences focused on various fiction genres. https://prowritingaid.com/

The Sapphic Quill: Website run by lesbian fiction author

Jae. The website provides advice for lesfic authors as well as many no-cost promotional opportunities.
https://thesapphicquill.com/
Wide For the Win: Facebook group focused on publishing widely. It still exists on Facebook but has moved a lot of discussion to Circle.
https://www.facebook.com/groups/5561866621558858
Writer Beware®: This is a phenomenal resource run by the Science Fiction & Fantasy Writers Association. Before you work with anyone, first make sure they weren't written up here.
http://www.sfwa.org/other-resources/for-authors/writer-beware/

ABOUT ELIZABETH ANDRE

Elizabeth Andre has been self-publishing lesbian fiction since 2014. She writes cozy paranormal mystery, lesbian romance, science fiction, and young adult stories. Before turning her hand to fiction, she was a newspaper reporter for many years and has the paper cuts to prove it. She has won many writing awards including a Goldie from the Golden Crown Literary Society for her fiction and a Peter Lisagor Award from the Chicago Headline Club for her journalism. She is a lesbian in an interracial same-sex marriage living in the Midwest.

Thank you for reading *Self-Publishing Lesbian Fiction, Write Your Own Way*. Self-publishing changes all the time. Scan the QR code below to access The Lesfic Self-Publisher and keep up to date on all things related to self-publishing lesbian fiction.